Christ

THIS BOOK BELONGS TO

Joanne Williams

AND CARRIES THE GOOD WISHES OF

AND **BirdWatcher's** DIGEST

P.O. Box 110 • Marietta, Ohio 45750
birdwatchersdigest.com

THE SEASONS OF THE ROBIN

Mildred Wyatt-Wold Series in Ornithology

THE
SEASONS
OF THE
ROBIN

BY DON GRUSSING

UNIVERSITY OF TEXAS PRESS 🐂 AUSTIN

Requests for permission to reproduce material from this work should be sent to:
Permissions
University of Texas Press
P.O. Box 7819
Austin, TX 78713-7819
www.utexas.edu/utpress/about/bpermission.html

⊗ The paper used in this book meets the minimum requirements of ANSI/NISO
Z39.48-1992 (R1997) (Permanence of Paper).

LIBRARY OF CONGRESS CATALOGING-IN-PUBLICATION DATA

Grussing, Don, 1939–
    The seasons of the robin / by Don Grussing. — 1st ed.
        p.   cm. — (Mildred Wyatt-Wold series in ornithology)
    ISBN 978-0-292-72120-3 (cloth : alk. paper)
    1. American robin—Life cycles.   I. Title.
    QL696.P288G78   2009
    598.8'42—dc22

                                                        2009024826

To Russell Galen
who believed this robin could fly

CONTENTS

PREFACE

IN YOUR YARD and neighborhood, wherever you live, high drama is under way right outside your window. Drama that most people don't see and seldom experience. It's wild and scary, involving creatures engaged in life-and-death struggles. Surviving storms and cold. Trying to keep from being killed or injured. Mating. Working to raise their family. Defending their home. It is a world of excitement, energy, and emotion. It is the world of wild creatures. And danger.

This book is about the uncommon life of one of the most common birds, the American Robin, a beloved symbol of spring. A bird that people interact with regularly without experiencing, wondering, or even thinking about the spine-tingling, nerve-wracking, adrenaline-flowing excitement that is so much a part of the life of every wild thing. Once you experience the world through a robin's eyes, I hope you'll look at every wild thing with new appreciation and with respect for what it accomplishes by living.

THE SEASONS OF THE ROBIN

PART I

INFANCY

1

SPRING

I F YOU COULD have looked in on the nest it would have appeared to be peaceful and quiet. Four light blue eggs were resting on a bed of soft, fine grasses and dog hair. The walls of the nest, formed from mud with grass, string, and a couple of bits of newspaper, were more than twice the height of the eggs. A kind of backyard adobe, they shielded the eggs from chilling wind and rain somewhat, though that was really the mother's job.

Mother was a female American Robin. When it rained, her job was to protect the eggs she had been incubating with her body. And she knew exactly what do, for this was her third season.

But she was off the nest now, as she often was at times throughout the day. She was busy feeding in the immense spread of lawn that rested below and to the west of the large oak tree in which the nest was located. And though the nest on which she had been sitting for the past two weeks looked peaceful enough to other birds that happened upon it in the middle of the lower branches of that oak tree, it was in fact the site of an exhausting struggle.

For a couple of days the birds inside the eggs had been preparing for it. As their nervous systems developed, as they became aware, if that is the word that describes development of their hearing, the only sense they could use as long as they were wrapped in the confines of a shell, they began to know their mother. They heard her whisper to them—a series of soft robin sounds. And they heard their father, too, and learned to recognize his sounds, both the soft clucks he exchanged with their mother when he would take over the nest-guarding duties and his songs. And what songs they were—loud from a distance, proclaiming his mastery over the half acre of suburban lawn, trees, shrubs, and brush that constituted his territory. Or the soft whisper song he made while singing in the tree near the nest. The whisper song was so soft that they could scarcely hear it, though they were within a few feet of their father.

But it was their mother, primarily, who had been signaling to them. And her sounds, combined with their development, led to the battle now taking place.

The four featherless, lizard-like, ugly baby robins were engaged in their first struggle for life. It was exhausting work. But slowly, regularly, each doubled-up naked baby would jerk its head, using the sharp tip on its infant beak to puncture and tear the shell that had protected but now constrained it. Like a hundred thousand generations of robins before them, they were cutting the shells with a circle right in the middle—the same place where many people crack a chicken egg when they break it open to cook it. But these baby robins were a lot neater, and a lot slower.

He was the first of the four to punch through the confinement of the egg. Of course, he didn't have a name. He never would. But he did have an identity, a strong sense of "self" that would serve him well when he needed it. For now, it is sufficient to know that he was first.

He was actually the second egg to be laid, though no bird or thing would ever know that. The fact that he was first out was testimony not to the time of his conception but to the strength he inherited. Here, as with every brood of young things, one was the strongest and one was the weakest, and he was the strongest. Thus he would be first in many things before these ugly, naked, and weak baby birds that appeared to be little more than skin-covered digestive tracts developed into graceful maturity.

Light came through his first tiny hole while his mother was off the nest, and the change he sensed but could not see made him work harder, twisting, lifting, and pushing his head to slowly, steadily enlarge the cut.

Soon he felt movement—he was always aware of movement—and sensed the darkness as his mother, making her soft sounds, settled briefly over the eggs, surrounding them with her feathers and exposing a warm, heat-producing patch of skin to the eggs. Ordinarily she would have turned them as she settled back on the nest, ensuring that they were evenly exposed to the heat of her body. But from the sounds within the eggs, she knew, both instinctively and from her past experience, that the activity going on there was important and demanded that they not be moved. It wasn't that the baby birds were warm-blooded creatures. They weren't; they relied on her heat for their body temperature, as they would for a few days yet until their own heat-producing and regulatory systems developed more. But turning the eggs now might confuse their efforts to get out. In effect, it was a birth in which the babies went through the labor.

She stood up on the rim of the nest frequently to observe the progress being made beneath her. And nine times during the day the father robin came to watch too, as she left to hunt, drink water from the birdbath on the other side of the yard, and bathe.

Finally, at four o'clock in the afternoon, he was out of the egg. His squirming and cutting had separated the shell into two pieces, and he could sense the brightness of this tremendous expansion of his world. As soon as he was free of the shell, his mother picked up half of it and flew across the street that was next to the oak, intending to drop it in a garden that was actually outside of the territory she shared with her mate.

The robin who "owned" that territory quickly flew in to intercept and fight her intrusion, but she simply dropped the shell, wheeled in a slow turn, and flew back to her oak tree, alighting first on a nearby branch to look for intruders in her territory before returning to the nest.

She was an alert, observant parent, and her experience had taught her to be on the lookout. There were many creatures that would delight in eating her, and even more that would rob her nest of its eggs or its young. Attempts had been made before. Trouble could happen again at any time.

Such odds would make a human being neurotic, but they simply made the robins alert. Those who weren't alert rarely lived long enough to produce any offspring.

Seeing nothing unusual, she hopped down three branches and then glided across the interior of the tree to her nest.

Landing on the branch where the nest was located created a movement that the baby robin immediately sensed. The movement made him want to lift his head and open his mouth, but he was too fatigued from his struggle to do it, and he dozed off instead.

Meanwhile, his mother flew with the other half of his eggshell to a spot on the lawn near the birdbath. For the rest of the afternoon and early evening, she spent her time brooding her emerging young to keep them warm and dropping their now useless eggshells in distant and obscure spots around the neighborhood.

It would be very hard for a predator to find the nest by the location of the eggshells.

By nightfall, Mr. and Mrs. Robin had a family.

The hard work was just beginning.

2

SPRING

H E COULDN'T SEE, but he learned the difference between his first
days and nights in many ways. Of course, he could sense light and
dark, but that didn't always have much to do with night and day. That was
because his mother spent much of the first few days of his life brooding
him, his brother, and their two sisters.

So the days were simply periods of light interspersed with periods of
darkness and warmth. And he came to approve of the dark periods, for his
mother's warmth and the nearness of her somehow made him feel good
and safe.

He also learned to know when the nights were coming by his father's
song. His father, whom he knew only as a voice and a visitor with food,
would always salute the coming evening with singing and battle.

On a typical night he would hear his father sing first somewhere to the
east of the nest. A snatch of song there, and he would move twenty yards
north, where he would sing again. He would hear his father mark with
song the approximate boundaries of his territory.

Twilight did not bring the long proclamations of the morning song,
but rather bits and pieces of song that seemed each night to be marked by
at least one territorial battle.

One night's fight might be caused by his father's trespassing on the
territory of the robin to the north, just across the street from the oak tree
containing the nest. It was an intentional trespass, part of a never-ending
attempt to increase territory and define boundaries. On another night it
might be a strange robin—who knows where it came from—landing right
in the middle of his father's territory. Such fights were much shorter than
the boundary squabbles with neighbors because this was a bird that had
deserted his own territory, perhaps because of the death of a mate, and
was in search of new grounds.

After these skirmishes started, his mother would usually leave the nest to join in the chase or defense and he would feel the damp cooling of late twilight. If the weather was pleasant she would be gone for quite some time, but eventually she would return to the nest. This last return, however, was different from any other of the day. That was because she would not bring anything to feed the infant birds when she returned. Instead, she would give them a quiet, scolding admonition and then she would settle down over them to protect them from the night and its dangers.

Most nights were totally uneventful for them. They would sleep comfortably warm, not knowing if she was keeping out the rain or just keeping the coldness of night from chilling their frail, featherless bodies. Without feathers as they were, even the chill of night could be dangerous. A cold rain would surely be more than their undeveloped, weak systems could handle.

But the night had other dangers too. In the early evening near the end of their first week, the safety of the brood was challenged. Even they became aware of it because their mother varied from her usual routine. Normally she made noise and stirred only at dawn. But that night the brood sensed danger as she tensed and rose slightly not long after she had settled down on the nest. They heard her hiss, kind of like a lizard or snake, and they heard her bill snap and click—new sounds to them, sounds that evoked considerable fear. But that was all they knew of the danger they were exposed to.

What they did not know was that a flying squirrel had leaped and glided from the elm tree across the street to the oak where their nest was. It landed on the tip of a branch about halfway down the oak and slowly worked its way up the branch, nipping at the green shoots of the oak tree and occasionally, luckily, capturing a delicious green caterpillar, one of hundreds that were dining on the oak's tender new shoots and growths that would become acorns in late summer.

As the squirrel got to the trunk of the oak, its claws made a noise that woke the mother robin. She blinked and tried to see the intruder. The flying squirrel's sharp black eyes caught the movement of her blinks, and it went to investigate. The squirrel was a female, heavy with developing young, and her body demanded protein. She had learned that she often found what she craved in birds' nests in the form of eggs at any stage of development, and even in the bodies of infant birds. She hadn't eaten an egg since the previous year when she surprised a Red-eyed Vireo off her nest in the topmost branches of a large elm tree. When the vireo flew, the squirrel quickly cut through two of the three freshly laid speckled eggs, eagerly sucking and lapping the juices into her mouth, looking very much like a wide-eyed child drinking a malt out of a large cup.

She had taken the third vireo egg with her back to her nest in an old Downy Woodpecker hole. And before morning she ate that too, and nibbled and swallowed part of the shell.

It seemed that fortune was going to smile on her again. She approached the robin hesitantly, uncertain as to whether she could frighten such a large bird off the nest.

Because the mother robin was awake, the squirrel had already lost one advantage, the opportunity to startle the bird into flight. As she approached the nest, crawling rapidly but cautiously out on the nearly horizontal branch, she became apprehensive. The robin was frightened. The squirrel was quick, creeping with jerky motions that were hard to see in the dark. But the robin could see it and she identified the intruder as a squirrel. She decided that she could defeat it. She rose off the nest slightly, her fear and anger causing her skin muscles to contract, raising the feathers of her body and making her appear quite a bit larger than she actually was.

But the squirrel kept coming, moving more slowly now, as it inched along the branch. Its tail was flicking, and it seemed poised and ready to fight.

The robin snapped her beak rapidly, clicking, sounding a warning to her enemy that she was prepared to defend her nest. Then she hissed and lowered her head for battle, thrusting her sharp beak at the squirrel.

It was too much of a risk. The squirrel quickly retreated along the branch and climbed to the top of the tree, where it darted out toward the tip of one of the small branches. Then it leaped and made a gliding fall back across the street to the trunk of the elm from which it had come. The flying squirrel scampered to a branch near the top of the elm and soared to a catalpa tree that edged the mixed stand of oaks and maples that was her home. In a little over a minute, the time it took the squirrel to move the fifty yards into the middle of the trees, she had almost forgotten about her near battle and had resumed her helter-skelter search for food and protein.

Mother robin, meanwhile, also forgot about the episode and dropped off to sleep. She did learn, though, and would never forget, that she could bluff a flying squirrel in a face-off at her nest. It was the kind of lesson that could one day mean survival for her young or her species. Such are the things that wild creatures learn.

Mornings erupted with a frenzy of sensory bombardment for the baby birds. Both within their bodies and from the outside world, drives and sounds dominated their environment. It was a time of great discomfort because of their hunger.

For one thing, they heard their father make a couple of brisk calls (announcing that he was awake) from his roost in the spruce tree near the small white house on the south edge of his territory. Every morning, just after he awoke, in the earliest faint light, he would make the short flight from the spruce to the television aerial on top of the house. There he would greet the dawn with his song.

The young robins' instincts told them that this was the language of their kind and they would never forget it. But robin songs are very individualistic. Like many species of birds, each robin adapts his natural song to his identity, nurturing the sounds from his repertoire that he likes, and repeating and changing them over and over. These favorite sounds are worked continuously into his songs, giving each robin a unique stamp of identity and individuality. The baby robin, his brother, and their sisters learned their father's song, as well as every sound that was in his language. By sound alone they could distinguish their father from every other robin singing the dawn song. And at dawn during this time of the year, every other male robin within hearing was singing.

Virtually every dawn was the same, the time of song initiation changing only if it was cloudy. Then singing started about fifteen minutes later and did not last quite so long, though on some cloudy and humid days the male birds would sing nearly all day long.

From day to day, however, there was little variation in the morning routine. Just as it began to get light, as the sky to the east showed the faintest soft presence of first light from the sun, their father would fly to the antenna, where he would scold. Then he'd fly to the telephone wires running parallel to the street beside the oak tree.

His first sounds of the day were not song but a kind of statement to his mate and offspring that he was awake—that he had survived another night.

With that, their mother would repeat the call and abruptly leave the nest. She was hungry (and her babies were absolutely craving food, so great was the demand of their rapidly growing bodies for protein and fluid). But she would tend to her needs first, for a weak mother is a poor hunter.

It was still too dark for many birds to be about, but the mother robins, descendants of woodland-dwelling thrushes, with eyes well adapted for excellent vision in poor light, were all on the grass hunting. Her mate, meanwhile, had now flown the ten yards from the wire back to the antenna, from which he could command a clear view of his territory and the sky.

There he would sing, a member of a mass chorus of robins, cardinals, and other early singers running the length of the meridian that marked the sunrise. Every male robin along that borderline between night and day would sing his song and fly from his first perch to the other perches that marked his territory, where he repeated his song. A proclamation of time and property. A statement of life and ownership, no matter how transient. A salute to freedom and living but also a tribute to the rules that governed the lives of all robins—indeed, all life.

To the father robin, it was his personal statement that mattered. To his babies, and his mate, this was the statement that made them feel secure.

As the robins started their day they heard the sharp "tisk-tisk" calls of a pair of Northern Cardinals nesting in a juniper about thirty yards away. Always awake at about the same time as the robins, the cardinals made a herky-jerky flight through the shrubbery beds to the bird feeder just outside the window of the house beneath the television aerial. There they would start the day with a handout of sunflower and safflower seeds provided for any guest, from pesky, quarrelsome House Sparrows to the bright cardinals and the handsome, dignified Rose-breasted Grosbeaks.

Shortly after the cardinals departed, Gray Catbirds would begin their peculiar calls, Brown Thrashers would sing their marvelous mimicry, and slowly the birds of more open areas would begin their day.

Many would awake with the outcry of the first robins. But they would sit drowsily, fluffed up and warm, until the sun rose higher, offering them more protection from the predators of the night as well as the visibility to see their prey.

After the chorus, father robin would join mother robin in searching the dewy grass for his breakfast. Hunters of opportunity, the robins took what was available—always looking for prized angleworms and night crawlers, especially in the morning, but taking whatever they could get—beetles, sow bugs, moths, katydids, caterpillars, worms, what have you.

After they had filled their stomachs so that the fronts of their breasts were plump and protruding, satiating their appetite, they began to hunt for their young.

What a day's work that would be! In the first part of the first week of the brood it wasn't too bad. The adults could quickly satisfy the babies. The young robins told their parents when they had had enough to eat. Not in words, of course, but by an easily recognized mechanism: a baby robin with a full stomach won't open its mouth, which prevents the dominant baby from getting all the food. This mechanism increased the likelihood that even the weakest of the four would get enough nourishment during normal weather to grow to adulthood.

So at first the small robins did not require much food. That gave the adults plenty of time to rest, and the father would take advantage of the time to splash in the birdbath at least twice a day and to sing, loaf, and preen his feathers.

But as the brood grew, the parents spent less time on themselves and more time trying to satisfy the growing appetites of the four gaping mouths.

To the young male, in the nest with his brother and sisters, it was a simple time. He would sleep with his head down, enjoying what warmth was available from the sun and the naked bodies of his brother and sisters. Then, when one of the parents landed on the nest or on the branch near the nest, the force on the moving branch would wake all four young. If he wasn't full, he would stretch his ugly naked head just as high as he could and if he was lucky, his mother or father—they both hunted equally hard—would cram a beakful of sometimes squirming things deep into his throat. (If they had stuck a rubber band in there instead of an earthworm he would never have known the difference until it obstructed his digestive tract.)

If he was full, he wouldn't put his head up so high, and he wouldn't open his mouth. At this time of year, late May, hunting was good, and his parents kept the brood well fed and frequently full throughout the first week of their life. The parents were busy, too, flying to distant areas of their territory with fecal sacs, the waste that the birds expelled. Like most perching birds, the robins were fastidious nest keepers and never allowed waste from the young birds to remain in the nest or on the ground below the nest. The young birds grew rapidly, and feathers began to emerge from their wings, tails, and over their entire bodies. And then, one morning nearly a week after the young robin had emerged from the shell, something happened to him. His eyes opened and he could see!

3

SPRING

H E FELT HIS USUAL morning discomfort. His mother flew off the nest while his father was singing, and he immediately missed the warmth of her body. But the coolness bothered him less and less each day as he, like his brother and sisters, grew his own warmth-holding feathers. And now his heat-producing system was working, too, keeping his inner furnace burning high (and using a lot of calories to do it).

But his feathers were neither out far enough nor thick enough to hold his body heat in. His wings were still more bare than feathered, and the quills of his primary feathers, the major flight feathers at the tips of his wings, were still largely enclosed. His rump and bottom too had more skin exposed than covered, but just the same, things were much better, comfort-wise, than a couple of days earlier.

That other discomfort, the emptiness in his stomach, was, if anything, more intense than it had been the day before. Each day as he grew he required more and more food. It was good that his feathers were growing so he could provide his own warmth, since his mother and father needed much more hunting time to meet the demands of the brood.

This particular morning was different because of what was happening to his brain, to his senses, to make him forget his hunger. Suddenly, new impressions were registering. In addition to all he could feel—the slight breeze as the warmth of the sun somewhere to the east began to heat the night air, the squirming of his brother and sisters—and the things he could hear—his father's singing somewhere toward the end of his territory and the clicking, raspy cries of a pair of grackles that passed to the south of the nest as they began their daily struggle to feed their brood—he could see more than just shades of light and darkness!

At first his vision wasn't sharp. But it was much more than the simple sensing of shades of light. He was rapidly aware of the great difference.

After his mother left the nest, the sudden cold shocked him to wakefulness. He snuggled up to his nest mates, and while doing that he executed the perfectly natural action that allowed sight. He opened his eyelids.

Daylight was slightly later and less intense on this day because it was cloudy. A warm front was approaching from the southwest, and the nimbostratus clouds that accompanied it delayed the light of morning somewhat, yet brought daylight faster than on a sunny day. That is to say, the sky became light faster than it did on a sunny day, but it didn't get light as early.

At first he could see just the light and fuzzy things all around him. Blobs and blurs. The big blobs seemed fixed; they didn't move at all. But the blurs were constantly moving—the waving motions of the large leaves on the branches of the oak above the nest.

A sudden blur accompanied by a rush of air and noise startled him. In the same instant his other senses told him that this was a familiar and good change. It was his mother bringing the first food of the day. Immediately he stretched his head as high as it would go and opened his mouth wide. Being the first to have his head up, the young male got the first mouthful of the day—a big fat night crawler that had left its hole during the night. His mother departed as quickly as she had arrived.

The young robin spent most of the morning alternating between feedings and trying to make his newly acquired sense work. By noon it was working well. The fuzziness was gone, the blurs had taken form, and he was rapidly soaking up images in his tiny brain, improving his vision with practice every waking second. At first, as the sharpness of his vision increased, he instinctively focused on moving things. The green oak leaves—yes, green, for like all birds he could distinguish color—fluttering as breezes would drift through the trees. From the first time he saw his mother, and associated her with her noise, he would be able to tell her from all other robins, until he was self-sufficient and no longer needed her.

But he quickly learned to recognize her and his father as they made their visits to the nest. And he could distinguish between them, though he didn't know how that happened.

He also began to study the passive things. The nest with dark mud and grass walls that still enclosed him. His brother and sisters, who now were also beginning to see. He could identify each of them as an individual, by subtle differences in the shape of their heads, eyes, beaks, and even their markings. And, of course, by their individual voice tones. Few humans, or birds other than robins, for that matter, would be able to tell the difference. But he could distinguish the differences, and they could identify him too, as the dominant bird of the four.

Each day the robin and his nest mates grew larger, crowding and pushing as the nest became tighter and more confining. And as they developed, their parents grew more and more excitable as they increased their frenzied feeding of the brood.

Soon he had grown large enough to peer over the side of the cup of the nest. That was how he learned he was high up—that there was space (a dimension he would master) beneath him and the secure platform that he was rapidly outgrowing.

Another thing he detected was the increased intensity of his mother's and father's reactions. They were quick to get upset. If a squirrel got too close to the tree, they would both go into a rage, diving at it and scolding until it fled from the commotion and bother. Grackles, chipmunks, cowbirds, and Blue Jays were harassed with the same ferocity. But the robins' method didn't work with all intruders.

On the eleventh day of life, as the young male was peeking over the side of the nest, eager to be first to sight mother or father returning with a beak full of squirming things, he saw a different sort of creature coming toward his oak tree. It was far bigger than any living thing he had seen before, but except for its size, it didn't seem particularly threatening. It walked on two legs like a robin, but it was more graceful and rhythmic. Something told him he should feel threatened, but something else made him keep watching rather than tuck his head down on his breast.

As the creature—a twelve-year-old girl with long brown hair, dressed in a pink sweatshirt, blue jeans, and tennis shoes—approached the nest, the young robin heard his mother scold and saw her fly from the lawn toward the girl, who had stopped, turned, and ducked, afraid of the attack.

His mother dropped a beakful of earthworms as she made her first swoop, and one of the worms landed on the girl's arm, startling her. Cries from the mother robin brought her mate to the scene, and he joined the dive-bombing attack on the amused but bewildered girl. Then it occurred to her that perhaps a nest was near, and she began to study the branches of the oak. She saw nothing.

So she took a few steps closer, and the intensity of the parental attacks increased. Their emotional scolding also attracted some curious grackles and jays from as far away as three hundred yards, intent on learning what all the commotion was about. They did not, however, join in the fight; they simply hopped and milled about the branches of the oak tree and nearby lilac bushes, observing the confrontation taking place below and giving warning cries in empathy. Other robins also flew in from their surrounding territories to learn the reason for the commotion. Those too far away to see flew to high perches to sit and scold. Baby birds were developing in nests throughout the neighborhood, and parent birds of all the early-nesting species were responsive to any threat as the young birds approached the time when they would leave the nest. That was because it was a time of great peril.

Ducking, holding her arm up to fend off the swooping attacks, the girl walked closer to the oak tree until at last she spotted the nest, just beyond her reach in one of the lower branches.

Then, since her intention was only to know where it was, she turned and walked back to her house, smiling.

Slowly the robins' anger diminished. And while they sporadically scolded for another five minutes, the birds were soon out on the lawn again, hunting for food for their young.

He had watched it all with interest, and he learned from his parents' actions that such big creatures were as much to be feared as the smaller intruders, though they didn't get nearly as close to the nest.

But soon the memory was locked away in his brain, to remain there until he needed it. He forgot about the whole thing and resumed his increasingly crowded life of eating, growing, and waiting for the forces of nature to act on him as he jostled with his brother and two sisters for room in the nest.

The next morning, shortly after the morning song, the nest suddenly became less crowded. He looked up, for this was very strange, and saw his sister perched on the side of the cup, facing outward. She had given up the jostling for room in the nest and simply climbed up, and it seemed to be a fortunate move.

Only a couple of minutes after she got there, her father flew to the branch on which the nest was built. She was closest to him, so she got the first feeding of the day. Shortly after that she got the second as well, because her mother landed on that same branch. She felt that she might knock her daughter off the nest if she tried to hop on the rim of the cup, so she took the nearest easy perch, which happened to be next to the daughter. The daughter got that squirmy meal, too, a pattern that was to continue for the next half hour until finally the young female was so full she couldn't open her mouth. Meanwhile, the other robins were so hungry they began to push toward their sister.

Being the strongest, he climbed over his brother and sister in the nest and ended up sitting on top of his brother. Then he flapped his wings and pushed with his feet to move toward his mother, who was half hopping, half flying through the branches of the oak tree with another meal of worms and insects. His fluttering wings caught his sister off balance, and the force knocked her backward, off the rim of the nest and onto his brother, who was also squealing in hunger at the sight of his mother. But the strong young male robin ended up with the meal.

As he was swallowing, he saw a quick movement above him that his mother spotted at the same instant. Instead of pushing the rest of the worm into his open mouth, she leaped up, screaming and flying almost straight at the intruder in their tree.

The big crow had sneaked into the oak tree, attracted by the commotion in the robins' nest. Somehow the predator had avoided detection by the watchdog jays and grackles.

Now the young robin's father attacked the big bird too, and the baby bird looked at it in terror. The crow was the biggest bird he had ever seen, and it had a huge black beak that it pointed at the furious, frenzied robin parents.

His father actually struck the crow a blow on top of its head—a blow that broke the skin, knocked out a few small feathers, and started a trickle of bright red blood. But it wasn't enough. The crow hopped down four branches and then walked out on the branch that held the nest.

Noise was everywhere. Blue Jays were calling from close and far away as they homed in on the terrified, screaming robins. And Common Grackles were all over the tree, joining the robins as they dived at the crow. Poking and jabbing his bill at the annoying songbirds, the crow stopped on the branch about two feet from the nest. It was his way of surveying the situation before making a move.

The door to the house across the yard from the great oak flew open and out ran the girl, her long brown hair streaming behind her as her eyes sought the cause of all this bird commotion. She thought, perhaps, that one of the boys from down the block was walking beneath the nest, just as she had done. But no one was in sight.

Seeing the girl, the crow quickly acted. He hopped to the nest in an instant. The terrified baby robins tried to duck deep into the security of the nest bowl. But they were too big.

Pain! The crow poked his big, sharp beak at the young male, making it squeal, a terrible, pitiful sound that sent the parents into an even greater rage. The pain grew suddenly worse as the crow picked him up by his wing, but his squeals brought the mother to the rescue, and she slashed the crow just below the eyes with her beak. In anger and defense the predator thrust his beak at the mother robin, dropping the young male. He cried loudly as he fell straight down and hit the ground with great force. It knocked the breath out of him.

The girl saw the young robin fall and ran toward the tree.

Angry, and afraid that he would get nothing, the crow prepared to flee from the approaching human. But he made one last thrust toward the nest and grabbed the young robin's sister in his strong beak. Then, without a chance to kill the young bird, the crow pushed off from the branch, flying away with slow, deliberate wing beats, the screaming, terrified young robin firmly in his grasp. The girl threw a rock at the crow. And the father robin, several grackles, and two Blue Jays chased it, scolding. But the crow headed south, annoyed by the commotion he had created and angry because the bird he carried was still screaming. He tried to shift the position of his captive in his beak and accidentally dropped it.

At that, he dove and wheeled in a tight turn to intercept the falling bird, this time catching it more firmly in his beak. As he turned again toward his nest, he crushed the young bird, silencing it. At the same time his pursuers, themselves rapidly flying away from their home territories, lost interest in the chase and, one by one, turned sharply around to return to their own nests and babies.

Steadily, directly, the crow flew to his nest. He too had babies, growing rapidly and demanding protein. The young robin would be ripped apart and would feed only two of the crow's three babies.

Back at the oak tree, the robin parents were still startled and furious, for now the human creature had picked up the strongest baby robin from the ground and was carrying it off to the garage. But she quickly returned with a stepladder and put him back in the nest, then went just as rapidly back to the house to pacify the distraught parents.

In fifteen minutes the backyard scene had returned to normal. The robins were feeding their three remaining young. They didn't seem to miss their absent daughter. The strongest robin got fed and began to feel better, though he had a strange discomfort in his left wing.

And a little girl told a strange tale to her father when he got home from work that evening.

4

SPRING

WHEN THE YOUNG male awoke on the morning of the fourteenth day of his life, he sensed that something was very different. There was excitement in the air, a nervousness that he could feel. Somehow he knew it was to be a big day for him.

Since the day after the first time he gained his sight his mother had no longer slept on the nest. Instead she slept near the trunk of a pyramidal arborvitae that grew alongside the door of the house where the little girl lived. Her fully feathered young no longer needed her body heat, and the nest was getting uncomfortably crowded as the robins grew.

By that time he, his brother, and his sister were fully in sync with the biological world of the robin, and they woke with their parents each day as the first light of dawn made seeing easy for their large black eyes.

But this morning was different. His father still sang, but the song was brief. And his mother hunted just after she woke up, but instead of bringing food to the nest, she remained on the lawn. Usually she went back to the nest right away. But today she dallied. She ate her fill on the lawn first where he could see her. He watched intently as she ran through the dew-laden grass. First she caught a gray moth. She pulled the wings off it, as she always did, and then ate it herself. Then he saw her catch and eat a beetle, two leafhoppers, and two earthworms.

His father flew toward the nest while his mother splashed in the birdbath near the house and drank from it. He brought a big worm with him as he flew to the branch of the oak and hopped along it to the nest. Abruptly, however, he turned and flew to the garden with the worm still in his mouth.

The young robin was puzzled by this behavior, and the fact that he was very, very hungry didn't improve his disposition. As he watched his father, his mother flew up behind him. Quickly he turned and opened his mouth wide, loudly squealing his infant plea for food, quivering his wings in excited begging. But his mother half leaped and half flew over the nest to a small branch above it. There she stood and watched the nestlings. In a series of soft calls she urged them to join her. At the same time, the father flew back to the tree, perching on a different branch about two yards beyond the mother. He, too, coaxed the nestlings, urging them to leave the nest, tempting them with dangling bits of food.

Somehow the parents knew that this was to be the day. For a couple of days their young had been climbing onto the rim of the nest, taking cautious steps out on the branch, flapping their wings. Today the birds sensed that they would have to go to their parents to get fed. They wanted to go to them, but they were very reluctant to leave the nest, which had been their world, their security, and their safety for their entire existence.

The strongest robin was the first to go. It was preordained. His strength, his size, his eagerness gave him the confidence to take this important move. He was extremely hungry. And he was ready to leave the nest. He had been practicing flapping his wings on the cup of the nest and he felt a sense of power in his breast. He felt strong. He knew he had the power to lift his body into the air when he flapped his wings.

But to actually leave the nest—to do it—made him afraid.

He hopped to the cup of the nest, and then to the branch forming the fork that held the nest. He looked down. Though it was high, it didn't frighten him. Slowly he started to walk and flap along the branch toward his mother, who was sitting ten feet away with a worm. She came to meet him, and as she got near he quivered his wings and begged for food. She approached him and crammed the worm into his mouth as if to silence the begging trill.

In a minute his father came and fed him also, but only after he had struggled a bit farther along the branch. It seemed that he had done the right thing in going to his parents, for now they were feeding him.

Back at the nest, his brother and sister were working up their courage. They grew increasingly excited at seeing their nest mate being fed while they had nothing. First his sister clambered to the cup of the nest. She inched out onto the branch where he sat and in a couple of minutes got her first feeding of the day, a squirming mass of mixed worms and insects. Relenting somewhat, the father robin brought a squirming green caterpillar to the other young male, who was still clinging to the side of the nest.

Meanwhile, out on the branch the strongest robin saw his mother on the lawn and felt a strange urge to go to her with his hunger. But conflict-

----

ing with that drive was an urge for protection—he very deeply needed to be near or in cover, and he felt a tremendous fear of leaving the shade and protection of the branches over his head.

But almost before he could think about it, he felt his still underdeveloped feet push him off the branch. In the same motion he stretched his wings into a downward-rearward push that combined with the thrust from his feet to propel him into the air.

It was the same impulsive behavior that a child experiences the first time he or she jumps off a dock into the water. It was a decisive moment that every young bird experiences. It was his first move into the world that separates birds from all other creatures except bats and insects—mastery of flight.

This flight, though, was a long way from masterful. The mechanical control of the breast and back muscles that powered his flight was instinctive, but directional control required thought and experience. When a bird flies, it is not simply making random movements. Navigation and direction require thought. A bird is flying from one particular place to another particular place, a destination. It has to know where it is going, and it has to know how to get there.

His first flight was clumsy. Although he instinctively knew what equipment to use to fly and navigate, he was utterly untrained in the fine points of flying. And because he was a robin, a species that leaves the nest before flight feathers and muscles are well developed, he was working inefficiently compared to many other bird species. As he left the tree, he aimed to the south, across the lawn toward his mother. He felt confident in a way, yet extremely insecure in another. He felt a sense of exhilaration as he propelled himself through the air, about five feet above the ground.

About halfway through his initial thirty-yard flight, he abruptly noticed that he had deviated from his course. He was going to overshoot his mother by about ten yards. He panicked. He felt unable to land, so he changed his plans and headed toward a green ash tree that stood some ten yards farther to the southwest. He was approaching too low, so he lowered his little tail somewhat to change the angle of his attack, and he instinctively changed his stroke to drive him up as well as forward.

But panic was as much in charge now as instinct, and because of fear he aimed his feet toward the first branch he focused on. But it was too late. He overflew it. So he clumsily stuck his feet out toward the next one, and one of his little claws got a good hold.

As most bird landings go, it was a failure. For him it was a small miracle. Somehow, after much wavering, grasping, and wing flapping, he got his other foot on the branch and squatted down—a movement that gives all perching birds security. When they squat, a tendon snaps across the bone in what is actually the heel of their foot, locking their toes into a grasping position. As the young robin felt his toes lock onto that branch, his three forward toes nearly meeting his strong rear-facing toe, he felt secure, tired, and, as usual, hungry.

So he celebrated his first flight with a loud, trilling squawk, a new sound in his vocabulary but one that his mother recognized instantly. These squawks, which he and his brother and sister would utter for the next few days of their lives, were her best means of keeping track of her brood, as they would never again be united in such close proximity as they had been in the nest. In fact, there was a good chance they would never share the same tree for any length of time for the rest of their lives.

• • •

There is great survival value in having these weak, nearly defenseless birds separate. A predator might catch one, but it is unlikely that three will get caught if they are in different locations.

Shortly after he squawked, he saw his father fly to him from beneath the overturned earth in the shrubbery bed at the front of the house. He squawked again and begged by fluttering his wings. His father flew directly to him, stuffed a fat white grub down his throat and left to resume the hunt.

His sister chose that moment to begin her first flight and flew smack into the side of the house. Luckily, she was going so slowly that the impact and the subsequent fall did not seriously injure her. She happily spent the rest of the day on the ground beneath the protective overhang of a spreading juniper. She got plenty of worms and bugs that day and was so full that she actually fell asleep several times.

It took until noon for the young robin's brother to work up the proper combination of nerve and hunger to push off from the side of the nest. When he did, his effort was certainly the most admirable in intent, though the worst in execution. For some reason he decided to fly straight west, climbing immediately toward the higher branches of a hundred-year-old elm that stood next to the driveway of the house.

But midway through his flight, a grackle flew past about ten yards over him, startling the young bird into a sudden but wobbly diving turn to the south. In a panic, he saw that he too was heading for a collision with the wall of the house, so he put all the energy he had into a steep climb toward the roof. He stumbled onto the midpoint of the roof in an awkward flutter, but then he could not figure out how to stop himself on the steep incline of the cedar shingles. He slid down, finally plopping to rest in the metal gutter. Fortunately it was dry. And there he sat for several hours, alternately squawking, swallowing the bountiful supply of insects and worms that his parents brought, and napping contentedly in the warmth of the afternoon sun.

By nightfall, the young female had hopped up into the protective branches of the arborvitae where her mother sometimes slept. The little male dropped from the gutter to the ground, where he slept under an overhanging lilac bush that had just gone into blossom. And the strongest of the brood hopped and climbed several branches higher in the ash tree. He finally fell asleep, but woke several times during the night, insecure without the warmth of his nest mates.

He would welcome the dawn now more than ever.

5

SPRING

Dawn came late the next day. It was cloudy, the kind of quiet, hot, muggy morning that announces the dreary promise of a flat, torpid, rainy day. And the robins reacted that way to it. Their morning song period was short. Adult birds throughout the area quickly got to the task of feeding their young.

The young robin was one of the first juveniles in the area to be off the nest. That was a factor not so much of his ability or his parents' experience as simply good luck. Blue Jays were very common in the oak, elm, and maple woodlands that made up the native vegetation of his home territory, and they caused some very important delays in the reproductive behavior of the early-nesting robins.

Part of the problem was that oak trees were a dominant species. They got leaves just a bit slower than elms, maples, box elders, and black cherries. But robins, tied into a biological reproduction cycle that didn't coincide with the emergence of oak tree leaves, sometimes built nests at oak tree locations that were very exposed.

Nest robbers of all sorts sought out the robin nests. The most persistent attacks (and the most harmful) were those made by Blue Jays. At that time of the year they abandoned their role as the noisy clowns of the woods and assumed a furtive, quiet posture as they prowled through the trees searching for robin nests.

When they located a nest, a pair of jays sometimes would check on it for several days if necessary, waiting for a moment when the laying or incubating mother was off the nest and the father was not guarding it. When they had a clear approach, they would consume the eggs or kill and eat the small young, sometimes just cracking the skull and eating the brains as though they were the seed of a sunflower. This year jays were successful in robbing nearly one-third of the early nests (in oaks) of eggs or young. But robins lucky enough or smart enough to build their nests in evergreens were usually the first to have broods leave the nest.

For some reason, Blue Jays never had a chance to see or attack the young robin's home on the oak; only the crow was successful in disrupting the efforts of his parents.

This was partly the result of a diversion created by man's interference. In the back of the lot containing the oak tree, a young man had several years earlier constructed a large, twelve-compartment birdhouse. It was mounted on a tall pole and was intended to be a home for a social, aerodynamic swallow called the Purple Martin. But after a few years, the man's wife died and he moved away. The family who purchased the home knew the martin house only as a birdhouse and did not maintain it or take it down for the winter months. Consequently, it was soon overtaken by House Sparrows, noisy, gregarious birds that packed each compartment with their nests. The combination of nests, the sparrows' early nesting habits, and their protective aggressiveness drove the martins away from the site.

But since House Sparrows, like robins, are early nesters, they came under the watchful eye of the local alert and hungry Blue Jays. Intelligent and adaptable, the jays didn't take long to learn that the martin house contained sparrow eggs and young. Of course, the sparrows were substantially smaller than the jays and thus were easy prey. The jays regularly hopped along the ledges of the martin house, sticking their long beaks into the compartments in search of sparrow eggs or young.

In fact, the jays established a flight lane, a kind of aerial highway, that led from a spruce tree at the back of the martin house (to look it over before moving in), to the martin house, and from there about fifty feet to the east of the robin's nest in the oak tree, across an open area toward other young trees that grew in a dense thicket.

The jays' habit of regularly checking the sparrow nests actually kept them away from the young robin's nest, for they usually got the egg or baby bird they sought from the sparrows. With a full beak and parent sparrows in a kind of halfhearted pursuit, their only goal was to fly clear of the area and take their prize someplace where they could eat it in peace. They never saw the robin nest.

The young robin paid little attention to his parents' reactions to the hot morning. But he did feel hunger deeply and squawked his loudest call to tell his mother where he was and that he was hungry.

A few minutes later he heard his sister squawk her call from the arborvitae bush. And about two minutes after that, his brother uttered his squawk from his damp resting place in the grass beneath the lilac. There was no justice. His brother got fed first.

The day turned out to be as dull as the dawn had promised. It was cloudy all day, and the young birds spent their time much as they did while on the nest, alternating between napping and eating.

In a series of slow moves the young male gradually edged out on his branch, finally losing his balance about three o'clock in the afternoon. Instead of falling, he flew across the yard and landed on top of a basketball backboard, mounted on a metal beam next to the driveway. He stayed there until about five o'clock, then flew, on his own initiative, to an elm tree, where he would likely spend the night.

His sister left her place in the arborvitae and alternately flew and hopped the opposite way, across the lawn to a clump of peonies that were in a small flower garden not far from the nest.

His younger brother stayed on the ground most of the day, flying only once, in early evening into a dense juniper bush that would be a perfect roosting spot.

It had been a good day for worm hunting, perhaps because of the dampness and humidity, and the three young birds were very well fed and rested. They were so full, in fact, that it caused their mother considerable consternation. That was because, like the young of all animals, the baby robins were totally self-centered. As the day wore on, their mother and father often lost track of them—because they forgot where they were, or more often because they didn't notice when the young birds hopped or flew to a new location.

So, on the eve of this good day of hunting, it suddenly struck the mother that she did not know where any of her baby robins had gone. Excited and agitated, she scolded often and flew to several places in her territory, flicking her tail, calling loudly with the sort of "help-help-help, please-please-please" calls that tell all robins there is trouble.

But her babies didn't answer. They were sound asleep! She became even more agitated, and her mate joined her in scolding and searching the territory. Within minutes every robin in hearing distance was nervous and alert, for the robin parents' calls told all of them that there was trouble about.

Finally the father robin flew to the elm tree in his search and discovered the young male there. As the young robin heard his father fly into

----

the tree, he opened his eyes. But he was still full and comfortable, so he didn't utter a sound or, except for a quiet yawn and a slow blink of his eyes, move a muscle.

It was the robins' way. Parents had to find their young. At this stage in their life the young birds didn't care about their parents as long as their needs were satisfied.

But then his sister squawked. Suddenly she was awake and hungry. That made his brother squawk. And in about ten minutes he squawked, too. The parent robins went back to work, and the robin restlessness that had taken over the neighborhood died down just as suddenly as it had started. Things were normal again.

That night, in typical late-spring fashion, a moderately strong thunderstorm passed through the neighborhood, with lightning and heavy winds. The young male robin was well protected by the elm tree, and he weathered the storm without trouble. It was his first night alone in the rain, and it proved that his instincts were working properly. As the wind came up, he turned around on the branch to face into the storm because that position made him feel more comfortable. The drops of rain that blew through the elm leaves hit him and woke him often during the storm, but his feathers were well oiled and the rain beaded up and rolled off, never leaving moisture to chill him.

Compared to the previous night, he wasn't as afraid either. He seemed to know that it was his way to always be alone from this day on.

The brisk northwest wind that followed the thunderstorm was typical of the continuing battle between colliding Canadian and Gulf air masses over the midwestern United States. It quickly dried the moisture it had helped create, however, and the robin family awakened the next day to the clearest of skies. It was the kind of day that, no matter when it comes, reminds you of autumn. No clouds. A coolness and a refreshing quality in the air that hints at the scent of spruces, pines, balsams, and yellow leaves of aspen.

As the first rays of sunlight sneaked into the dark of night, the young robin opened his eyes and looked around. He was hungry, and he felt a need to move. He fluffed his feathers and opened one wing at a time, stretching out to his full length. It felt good. He turned his head to touch behind his wings, and in a most uncoordinated manner tried to arrange and sort the feathers at the junction where his wings merged with the softer, thicker, downy feathers on his back.

Then, when he was through (feeling as though things were somehow in order for him), he leaped from the branch and flew toward his father, who was alternately running, listening, and watching the ground on the lawn below. His landing was rough. He would have to make many flights before he would master the art of almost completely halting his airspeed before extending his feet to touch the earth. Instead, the young robin literally flew onto the ground, surviving because of his light weight and the resilient construction that all young creatures have.

Immediately upon regaining his composure, he hopped and ran after his father. He felt confident enough now to expose himself in the open. And somehow he knew he would get more food if he stayed near his parents while they hunted.

His brother and sister had the same idea, and soon the entire family was on the lawn, the youngsters staying within ten or fifteen feet of one or the other parent, begging loudly every time a worm was pulled or a bug snatched from the earth. This was to be the pattern for the next few days: the youngsters following their parents everywhere they went.

Each developed in several ways each day. For example, by the start of the third day each was making much better takeoffs and landings. Of course, their tail and wing feathers had grown each day, improving their flying power and maneuverability. And the exercise and protein encouraged the breast muscles to swell. These largest muscles on a bird's body responded readily to the demands of flight and abundant food supply.

Each was also learning about the concept of what was good to eat and how to catch it. Of course, none of them had caught a worm yet. Worms were the most difficult prey of all for a young robin. But they had seen other things moving in the grass. The young robin finally tried to pick up a little green worm that had fallen out of an oak tree. He couldn't quite put his bill on the squirming thing. And his inexperience really showed, for he eventually lost sight of the worm in the grass. He simply forgot about keeping his eye on it. But gradually he was catching on. And with each hour he caught a little more food by himself, as did his sister and brother.

One day their mother seemed preoccupied with another task, and they followed the pattern that had been developing, staying with their father. Their mother had been doing less and less hunting for them. On this day they noticed that she was carrying pieces of grass and mud from a puddle in a driveway across the street to a fork in the arborvitae where she often slept.

So they promptly forgot about her, and she forgot about them.

Their father continued to hunt for them, but since he was alone now in this effort, the young robins were forced to rely more and more on their own resources to fill the stomachs beneath their speckled breast feathers. And by and large they were successful.

Each hour with their father was beneficial and taught them more about how to eat and what was good to eat. It wasn't long before they learned why robins run. Hopping along after their father never really gave them a chance to see the tip of an earthworm hidden in the soil beneath the tangled roots of grasses and weeds in the lawn. However, when they started to mimic their father (while also following a deep-seated, instinctive urge to run), they often saw, as soon as they stopped, slight movement in the soil beneath the grasses. It was as if their sudden approach (and perhaps the vibration from the running) caused worms that had tunneled to the surface to start back down.

The young robins obeyed their urge to grab at the movement and poked their sharp bills into the soil. Then began the tug-of-war that usually, but not always, resulted in victory for the bird. But worms and bugs weren't the only things the young robins learned to eat.

The three robins followed their father off the lawn into some taller, three-leafed plants with rough edges. They watched intently as their father ran up to a big red strawberry, sliced off a piece with his bill and with a bit of tugging worked it loose. The young male's sister got the first morsel, so he went after a berry that was a couple of feet away from his father. He plucked it with his beak and picked off a little slice. It felt good in his throat and in his stomach. So he ate another slice and another, until he had eaten half the berry.

They were learning other lessons in these days with their father as well. As the young male began to bite off another slice of berry, his father gave an abrupt warning call and flew toward the power line far across the street. The suddenness of his father's call and jump to flight brought his head up in fright. Then he saw a man thing running at him.

Quickly, he and his siblings flew, following the general direction their father had taken. This was the first time a man thing had seemed to be after him. He didn't think much about it, but it reinforced his instinct to flee from anything that appeared to be rapidly closing the distance between him and it.

As he flew, he looked back at the man thing, and he noticed that it had stopped running and was just standing there near the delicious berries. Braking with his wings and tail, he landed on the wire near his father and looked down at two other man things walking along the ground below, one big, the other smaller. His one eye glanced at his father, but his father didn't seem to be afraid of these man things even though they were very close. Perhaps it was because the man things were not looking at the robins.

So, somewhat puzzled, he just sat there and waited for his father's next move. In moments, as if on a signal, the four birds flew together to the small pond in the vacant lot just below the power lines.

There, each bathed in turn and then flew to the oak trees that grew near the pond. Claiming separate perches, they preened their feathers, carefully drying and arranging them after their invigorating bath. And then the youngsters and their father took brief afternoon naps, alternating the naps with more fluffing and preening.

Tonight, just before dark, though they didn't know it yet, they would make the longest flight of their lives so far. Their father was about to take them on another step toward their independence.

6

SPRING

THE SUN FELT warm and good to him. He was very content as he dozed on his perch near the pond. He heard an occasional brief scolding as the solitary male Belted Kingfisher that hunted there complained about missing a minnow. But mostly it was a cozy, comfortable nap, with his body turned to the rays of the sun.

A quiet "trup-trup-trup" from his father woke him up, and he saw his father, brother, and sister push off from their branches and fly up the steep hill that led from the pond back toward their territory. Of course, the young birds had no feeling of possession, no sense of territory. They simply went where their father went for the most part, though frequently they were not as quick to respond to his signals and changes of direction. Still, today, he was the guiding destiny of their lives.

The young male robin climbed steeply to clear the top of the hill, closed his wings for a second to shoot past a grapevine that had nearly strangled a small aspen tree just over the peak of the hill, and then carefully glided to the power line where his father, brother, and sister had landed a few seconds before.

They all looked around to make sure there was nothing dangerous in the air above or on the ground below, and then, almost simultaneously, they dropped from the line and set their wings to make a steep glide toward their home lawn.

They spent the next thirty minutes hunting in their territory, with the young robins catching more food themselves than their father fed them. Then they flew to an old cement birdbath placed near the picture window in front of the house. The father got to the birdbath first, then was joined on its rim by the young male. His smaller brother and sister landed on the lawn below the bath and stood there, watching and listening while their father drank, then bathed.

As his father gingerly hopped into the water (which was deeper than his legs were long and thus soaked the lower feathers on his body), he jabbed his beak and hissed at the young male.

The young bird was so startled by this behavior that he almost fell over backward. But then his father ceased his aggression and seemed to tolerate the young male's presence as he bathed.

His sister, excited by the splashing as her father repeatedly submerged his head in the water and then flapped his wings to work the clinging wetness under his feathers to his skin, flew to the rim once. But she felt nervous about landing with two robins already there, and so she flitted back down to where she had been standing.

After his father was finished, the strong young male performed his bathing ritual, dipping his head in the water and splashing it all about him, working it under his feathers with his wings. When he was done, he stood in the water for about twenty seconds and then flew with a great deal of effort to the ash tree where he had made his first landing after leaving the nest.

As he sat preening and ruffling his feathers, his sister and then his brother took their turns in the bath, finally joining their father in the low branches of the oak tree where they had hatched.

After all the birds had preened and dried their feathers, their father led the way to a patch of wild strawberries on the floor of the little plot of woods to the south of his territory. Each ate two of the small, tart berries.

Then, as quickly as they had landed, they took off again, following their father, who was digging his wings deep into the air and climbing rapidly. The somewhat weaker youngsters fell behind, with the strongest young male ten yards from his father, followed by his sister and then his brother.

In a few seconds they were higher than the young birds had ever flown before. It wasn't such a great altitude, really. There were Purple Martins, Barn Swallows, and Chimney Swifts coursing for insects far above them, but they were just above the tallest oaks and elms, and the openness caused the young birds to feel exposed and somewhat nervous. This was the first time they had been above all the surrounding protective cover.

Then they reached a comfortable altitude, just skimming over most branches but occasionally dropping down a bit and twisting and turning time and again to pass through the crowns of some of the tallest trees. Their father slowed a little. He settled into a cruising speed that permitted rapid flight without a great deal of energy expenditure. He used quick, powerful, but somewhat intermittent wing strokes like the ones robins use when migrating long distances. It was a beautiful twilight without an interfering wind. The birds moved along, excited and calling, in a staggered single file at a ground speed of thirty-two miles per hour.

When their father would get a little too far ahead, he would land, pausing just for a second or two, on the topmost branch of a convenient tree. He would give a reedy, drawn-out call, similar to the territorial challenge call, and then he'd push himself off with his powerful legs and with four or five deep strokes of his wings, accelerate quickly to cruising speed.

The stronger young male liked this game of follow the leader. He felt confident making the rapid, winding turns through the branches and leaves that broke through the top of the wooded canopy. And he felt comfortable with the sensation of speed and power as he raced past the topmost branches.

Once his sister pulled up along his left side, and as he glanced at her he saw, off in the distance, other robins flying in the same treetop-high manner, heading south as they were. Then he noticed a couple of birds off to his other side, about a hundred yards away. They were immature robins, like him. And they were heading in the same direction at about the same speed. The sight of these other birds excited him and spurred a desire deep within to be with other robins. But he still followed his father, for he didn't know what else to do.

They hurried along for about twenty minutes, pausing a couple of times for just a few seconds. It was the longest flight the young birds had ever made, and the effort was beginning to tire their unconditioned breast muscles. It hurt. But suddenly the land seemed to fall away beneath them, and just as quickly their father began to lose altitude. Beneath, the land sloped steeply toward a blue ribbon of water that curved and twisted like a gigantic worm through swampy earth. Straight ahead of their father was a vast stand of maple, aspen, oak, and cottonwood trees. From all sides robins were converging on this dense mini-forest, and even now, with the wind rushing over his ears and through his flight feathers, he could hear the calls of more than a hundred robins.

After a few braking flaps of wings, he and his father, brother, and sister landed in a tall aspen on the outskirts of the roost. His brother was tired, and immediately settled down as if to sleep, but his father called them to follow him, and the birds pushed off again, darting through the trees to the thicker roosting area at the center.

There they saw robins everywhere, mostly adult males and juveniles from the first hatch, with a few adult females scattered here and there. There was much scolding and calling, and it was all quite confusing to the youngsters. But they were very tired after their strenuous flight and quickly fell asleep in the late twilight, which seemed even darker than usual because of the dense canopy of leaves.

His brother and sister were about three branches below him, and his father was preparing to roost on a branch above and slightly to his right. Just as he dozed off, the strong young male heard a rush of wings and saw his father fly through the dark to a tree even deeper in the clump. But he was too tired to follow, and somehow he didn't seem to care whether he did or not. After all, he wasn't hungry.

He never saw his father again.

As tired as they were, the three birds had a restless night. Mostly that was because of the occasional scolding they heard as some nearby robin was awakened by a real or imagined enemy. But it was also caused by the strangeness of their surroundings—they sensed that a change had been made in their lives, but they didn't understand it at all.

Finally, dawn slipped through the heavy canopy of leaves, and the young birds watched the robins around them silently fly away. Though it was very dark, in about fifteen minutes most of the robins had gone, leaving behind a few unpaired adults and many young and now parentless birds like themselves.

Dutifully they remained near where their father had left them. But it didn't take them long to sense that he was gone. Besides, they knew they were fully capable of satisfying their hunger without their father's help.

To his left the young male saw three other robins, one adult female and two youngsters about his age, flying off to the northwest. He called to them and pushed off, climbing rapidly to clear the dense tangle of tree limbs and branches. The three robins were a hundred yards or so ahead of him and had climbed to about twice the height of the trees in the valley, an altitude that left them only a slight additional climb to clear the trees at the top of the bluff that was the boundary of the river floodplain. The young male didn't know where the three were going, but his instinct told him, because of the directness of their flight, that they did know. Somehow, he felt that with them he would be led to food.

The birds cruised for about ten minutes at treetop height toward a large chimney that jutted high into the bluish-gray predawn sky. It was an easily seen landmark that helped many birds in the area navigate. The three robins and their straggling companion were heading right at it.

As they flew toward the chimney, the young robin looked down, instinctively locating landmarks. To his left he saw a narrow ribbon of water, a small creek that wound through a suburban area from the general direction of the chimney. Without his consciously thinking about it, this navigational landmark was etched in his memory, as were the chimney and a water tower to the east of that.

The three birds reached their destination ahead of him and quickly lost altitude, alternately plummeting with closed wings, then repeatedly spreading both wings and tail to control the speed and direction of their descent.

The young robin mimicked the actions of the other three, but when they landed on a power line running through this complex of buildings and spacious grounds (which was a large public institution, formerly a tuberculosis sanatorium but now converted to a nursing home), he flew past them, landing instead on a no parking sign near the road in front of the main entrance to the grounds. He looked over the vast lawn before him, sparkling and damp with a heavy dew. It seemed safe, so he made a little glide and landed on the grass about five feet from the edge of the road.

His three guides flew off the power line, over the building, and out of sight. But he didn't care. He was an independent bird today. On his own. His brother and sister were on their own as well, though he never even gave them a thought.

PART 2

ADOLESCENCE

7

SUMMER

ONE OF THE FIRST lessons the young robin learned was that there was an abundance of good hunting areas. In summer, robin food was nearly everywhere. On the lawns, in shrubbery beds, in shady places, beneath the trees, and in the sunny places too.

His natural fondness for water led him to discover sprinklers, strange devices that sprayed water into the air so it could fall on grass like rain and bring earthworms to the top of the soil. So he spent much of his time during his first week alone looking for the sprinklers scattered about the sanatorium property. Every night he flew back to the roost by the river with growing numbers of other robins.

He made another important discovery that week. There were a lot of places where he was not welcome. He learned his lesson the hard way. It was his first afternoon on the grounds of the sanatorium. He had just finished a brief rest in one of the few surviving elms surrounding the main drive. As he opened his eyes, he heard the gentle "swish, swish" of water falling on grass.

Hungry, he looked in the direction of the sound and saw the water spinning from a sprinkler onto the shaded lawn about forty yards to his left. It was inviting, and he sensed that the hunting there would be good. He pushed off his roost, took a few quick wing beats, and then held his wings out for a long, gradual glide to the grass.

But just as he extended his feet to land, turning his wings up and spreading his tail down to slow his forward motion, he glimpsed a blur to his right. Suddenly he was struck a blow on his back. It sent him tumbling awkwardly to the earth. In an instant, his reflexes being so very quick, he regained his footing and turned to flee. But he made the mistake of looking around to see what had struck him, and pow, he was hit again and wrapped up in rolling, tumbling confusion by his attacker. As he rolled he saw that it was an adult male robin and that it was about to hit him again. This time he squatted and avoided the snapping bill. The young robin was overwhelmed by both the pleading baby noise he himself was making and the aggressive scolding of the adult bird. Somehow he broke loose and fled from the robin and its mate, which had just joined in the fight. Then, as suddenly as it had begun, the adults broke off their pursuit and landed on the ground, still scolding.

He landed too. He was confused and bewildered by this aggression. But he had learned. He knew that he didn't want to go through that kind of punishment again. And he sensed from the behavior of the pair that he was not to cross into their territory. From their reaction to his presence and from his inherited memory, he formed a general idea as to the size and the location of the boundaries of the property the adults were protecting, and henceforth he stayed out of it.

Succeeding encounters with other pairs throughout the area in and near the sanatorium taught him to watch for the approach of other robins whenever he flew to a new place.

But bits and pieces of good, unclaimed feeding grounds were still scattered everywhere. Besides that, it seemed that food grew more abundant with each passing day. There was no need for the young male robin to be particularly attached to one place, and thus each day he wandered throughout the grounds and beyond, returning three or four times a day to a leaky faucet near a maintenance shed to drink, and sometimes to bathe and preen. The faucet steadily dripped enough water to form a small permanent puddle on the clay-gravel driveway beneath it. Here the robin was often joined by several other birds in need of a drink or a bath—Chipping Sparrows, Common Grackles, European Starlings, House Sparrows, and a pair of Northern Flickers that were raising their young in a black cherry tree where the young robin sometimes preened.

As the days passed, the young robin wandered north beyond the institution grounds until finally, one morning, he overflew the chimney completely, landing instead in a residential area about a mile to the north.

It was now the fourth week in June, and already many adult robins that had successfully completed their first nesting attempts were nearing the last stages with their second broods. These early breeders might even have yet another nest attempt before cessation of the breeding cycle. Others, their first attempts interrupted by predation from jays, grackles, or other natural perils, would produce young birds somewhat later, resulting in a steady supply of juvenile birds of varying ages throughout the summer.

But the fourth week of June also marked the end of an unusually long period of mild weather with occasional light rain but no storms. That changed on the day the young robin chose to begin his wandering.

His morning flight from the roost was uneventful. Now, instead of following other birds, he was striking out on his own, and on many days he was joined by two or three other juveniles that would fly all or part of the way with him.

Sometimes birds just a couple of days younger than he was would follow him throughout the day, maintaining a discreet distance but remaining in his presence and, in fact, learning by mimicking his actions, hunting and interacting with territorial robins.

Today, however, he was alone, and since he was venturing into new territory, he was cautious and alert as he approached the prospective hunting grounds.

Skimming over the tops of the trees, he impulsively decided to land in a medium-sized red oak. There was no particular reason for his decision. It did not involve deliberation. It just looked like a good place to land. The young robin thought that perhaps the hunting nearby would be good. He surveyed the scene below while still looking about for predators in the trees or, perhaps even more important, the menacing attack of another robin protecting its territory.

He didn't see anything threatening in the immediate vicinity, so he called out twice, a kind of alerting action that would rouse any protective territorial robins nearby. But all he received in response was some mild scolding by robins far up the street, too far away to be protecting this piece of land. So he folded his wings and deftly dropped to a split rail fence that was directly beneath him. A few flaps of his wings slowed him down, and he landed gingerly on the fence. Once again he surveyed the scene around him.

The fence surrounded a small backyard. In the rear of the yard was a garden area that contained, among other things, plants he recognized immediately—strawberries! The young robin ducked instinctively as another robin passed some yards over his head, but the bird was just flying by and ignored the young male.

He hopped and flew to the ground beneath the fence, choosing to hunt his way across the lawn to the strawberries rather than to fly immediately to them. Instinct told him that was safer. It gave him a better opportunity to look over the surrounding bushes, and he needed to do that. He had every alert bird's built-in paranoia. He was always afraid that something was out to get him. And, to be sure, that was often the case.

The young robin ran a few steps and stopped, his eyes alert for movement both from the sides and from above and also in the grass below. But he saw no worms. He ran a few more steps. Stopped. This time a quick movement caught his attention. It was a small green caterpillar of a type he'd eaten before. He poked at it. It wasn't squirming much, so he picked at it twice to make sure it was dead and then swallowed it.

Forgetting momentarily about the strawberries, he changed direction and ran toward the center of the yard. He felt a need to have more animal matter in his stomach.

A couple of bits of sand attracted his attention, so he picked them up and swallowed them. While it was true that he didn't need as much gravel as birds that ate seeds (and thus had more grinding to do), the robin occasionally ate a few hard bits to augment the minute pieces of dirt that got into his gizzard from eating earthworms. The seeds of many of the berries he ate would also perform some grinding functions in his gizzard.

He ran a few more steps onto the lawn, but he found no earthworms there. It was a meticulous lawn, sprayed and fertilized with the most expensive materials available, and it had been subjected to several years of constant drenching with insecticides and crabgrass killers. It was an impossible environment for earthworms. And that was one reason why it was also barren of robins.

Sensing the futility of a hunt in this yard, the robin turned back toward the strawberries, flying low over the ground. Although small, the patch was a productive little piece of ground. The staggered plants with their three rough leaves and creeping system of runners were loaded with huge red ripe berries. The robin looked at one plant, decided that the berries on it were too big to handle, and ran a few steps to another plant. It had smaller berries, about the size of a man's thumb. They were too big for the robin whole but perfectly bite-sized if sliced with a sharp beak. He poked and pulled, and took a large morsel from one of them. Finding it satisfying, he performed a typical robin trick—he didn't eat the other half. Instead he probed into a different berry, swallowed more, and then moved on to two more plants, where he nipped at three more berries, taking flesh from each. So intent was he on this meal that he failed to look carefully under the branches of a recently planted spruce tree that stood to one side of the garden near the end of the strawberry patch. By the time he had reached his third plant, the young robin had traversed the length of the ten-foot patch and was about to turn and start back through it.

But then he saw something that made him stop as if paralyzed. He felt extreme fear, and his breathing actually stopped for a second. He had seen something that was almost hypnotizing, causing a confusing lack of action, a defense mechanism from his days in the nest that was now working against him.

He still hadn't identified the danger; he'd only sensed its presence.

This isn't to say he couldn't see it. He could see it, but he didn't know what it was. Under the spruce, just six feet from where the young robin stood, crouched a large orange-striped, short-haired cat. Not a tom but a smart, experienced female that was let out of the house every night "for exercise," according to her owners. And exercise to this cat meant killing. She was an active predator that averaged one kill every two days from spring until fall. Cardinals, grosbeaks, sparrows, warblers, orioles—any bird that came on or near the ground fell to her claws. Over the spring, summer, and fall she would kill nearly 150 birds. And now she was staring at this young robin, unblinking, unmoving, ready to lunge.

"Hey!"

The sharp yell startled the cat, and she jumped slightly while at the same moment turning her head toward the noise.

Three things startled the robin. In one instant his right eye saw a man thing running at him and waving an arm. With that eye he also saw a clump of dirt flying at him. With his other eye he saw the cat react to the noise. Immediately he turned and flew away from the threats, screaming and scolding in his most frightened voice.

He climbed steeply to a high telephone line that ran from the alley behind the garden to the house. The young robin was so intent on what was going on behind and below him that he almost missed the power line with his feet. The cat had wheeled and turned away from the man and was racing down the alley to her home.

The man, a retiree with white hair, stopped, surprised at the sight of the cat. A hint of a smile came to his lips. He looked up at the robin, still tottering on the swaying power line.

"Okay, fella, it looks like I saved your life. Now please stay out of my berries."

The robin watched the man go into the house and remained on his perch for about a minute. Then he heard a familiar sound from the direction in which the cat had run.

It was a low, monotonous call of scolding and caution—a higher note and a lower note, repeated several times, notes that meant ominous things for all robins. He sensed the danger in the low, mournful call and flew up the alley to investigate, landing again on the power line. It wasn't hard to see what was happening. Several robins were sitting on high branches and power and phone lines, territorial fights temporarily put aside. On the ground below walked the same orange cat, oblivious to the attention being paid to it. A young robin just out of the nest hung from its mouth.

From time to time one of the dead bird's parents would change from the ominous "predator on the ground" call to a brief, high-pitched scolding. And a few grackles and starlings had joined in the scolding with their own excited, worried, nervous sounds.

The young robin joined the chorus too, echoing the robin sound that would disturb all robins all their lives. But soon the cat walked into an open garage to eat its prey and the birds forgot the fear and depression, quickly returning, as birds do, to the important tasks of caring for themselves and their young.

The robin stayed on the power line for a few more minutes. He became very still and quiet as the heat of the day built up. He waggled his tail feathers a couple of times, called out, and proceeded north. This area didn't suit him at all.

SUMMER

THE PATH THE YOUNG robin took followed the stacked rows of eight power lines that ran from pole to pole along the alley. He flew just higher than the poles and sped past the lines of garages at a rapid thirty-five miles an hour. Soon the alley ended at a road, and beyond the asphalt stood a large expanse of grass in front of a junior high school. While that looked like a good place to hunt, the young robin could see beyond to what appeared to be a better site farther north. It was a vast green area with trees, shrubs, and ponds, and his keen eyes detected huge sprinklers everywhere. So he decided to go there and flew over the school and the busy four-lane highway that ran beside it.

He felt a certain uneasiness in his system. It was not related to the cat incident but was more a general discomfort that he'd known before. Usually it was accompanied by rain showers, but his feeling today seemed to portend something more intense, more ominous. It didn't stop him, though. He was hungry, and the feeling even intensified his hunger. He began to drop from his altitude just as he crossed the highway, though he still had a good two hundred yards of church parking lot and a pond to cross before entering the green area. Gradually he dropped lower and lower, until the final thirty yards of his flight were just inches above the pond that was on the edge of this vast area.

But before landing on the grass, he dropped his tail into the air stream and quickly climbed five feet to land on a post so that he could take a look around. Actually he had landed on a rectangular board that had been nailed to the post. The board was bright orange and had black letters on it that read: out of bounds—replace all divots.

To the robin this golf course appeared to be an ideal hunting spot. There were great expanses of grass. Some of the grass was kind of long, in other places it was shorter, and in other areas it was very short indeed. On a hill to his right he saw a scattering of other juvenile robins and a few adults too. He flew toward them.

The robins were feeding in a loose group with about thirty feet between birds. Most of them had nearly satisfied their hunger already, and they paid little attention to this latecomer. He looked around at his companions and then began to hunt. Run a few steps. Stop. Pause. Look for motion. Listen. If there is any noise or motion, investigate. Otherwise, run some more.

After about fifteen minutes the young robin's stomach bulged comfortably and he felt a need to drink. He flew to an oak tree at one side of the fairway and wiped both sides of his bill clean of the dirt and slime left over from the worms he'd swallowed.

Then he looked for water. The pond he'd flown over on his way to this fine place was closest, so he flew back to its shore. It looked shallow, and the young robin was cautious as he edged into the water. But his hesitancy changed to near madness once he got in. He ducked his head under, sending the water down his back while opening his feathers and splashing more water against his sides with his rapidly fluttering wings. His whole body was moving as he splashed and ducked and sloshed around in the water, attempting to get every feather wet and washed free of dust and dirt.

Twice he hopped out of the pond as if to fly away, but both times he hopped back in, as though to make certain that he was doing a good job.

The third time, he was completely soaked and he knew it. He hopped out of the water and then flew (with a great deal of effort because he was heavy with water and aerodynamically inefficient since his feathers were disarranged) to a clump of white birch trees that looked like good cover. There he perched on a limb and spent the next ten minutes preening, oiling and arranging his feathers, chasing off a couple of lice that annoyed him from time to time, massaging his skin where it itched and where it felt good.

Finally he finished. As he rested he became aware of that strange tense feeling again. By this time the heat had spawned huge white cumulus clouds that were building and swelling high above him. Uneasiness was in the air as the wild creatures felt the barometer falling and sensed the approach of the first severe storm of the summer.

The young robin knew something different was happening, but he didn't know what. It was obvious to him that other robins sensed the same ominous things. All the territorial adult males for as far as the robin could hear were singing and scolding nervously, too.

Back at the feeding spot on the hill, he saw the other young birds showing their nervousness. As he flew up, four of them called and started into the air, flew about five yards, landed, and scolded each other. Then several others on the hill took off and called, flying about twenty yards. The young robin joined in this nervous behavior and trailed after the second group, dashing low to the ground to the top of the hill. Then he landed, facing west. From there he saw it coming.

A fast-moving line of black clouds was rolling out of the southwest, stretching from horizon to horizon and as high as he could see. He was startled by it, and though nothing in his experience had taught him anything about storms, his inherited memory told him that the black thing coming toward him was definitely a threat to his survival. He attempted to fly toward the storm to get to a tall blue spruce that looked like it would provide cover. But when he was about halfway there, he met the wind rolling out ahead of the downburst.

It was fierce and strong. He tried to drop close to the ground to escape it, but that was impossible. He folded his wings to lower himself, but the wind started to blow him over onto his back. In defense he opened his wings to the wind, letting it catch and turn him. Then, with the wind blowing him sideways, he flapped with all his might to turn his body so the wind was at his back. Twice it almost rolled him upside down, but finally, after more flapping and maneuvering with his tail, he was flying with the wind. He was just flying now, not going to any particular place, just flying for his life. Trying to get away from the storm. Trying to stay in control. Trying to stay alive.

He was trapped in the leading edge of the squall line that was moving from southwest to northeast at about fifty-five miles per hour. Unable to land, and fearful of changing direction, he flew within the line, ahead of the rain and hail, struggling to maintain his stability in the violent air. He was rapidly being blown away from all familiar territory.

He passed over lawns and houses, freeways and roads. Gradually the character of the land beneath him changed. At first there were square fields and farms and he could see men and dogs scurrying to get out of the storm's way. Lights came on at gas stations and in towns as the darkness that was just behind the wind enveloped the land. But after he'd been in the air for an hour, there were few lights below. The land still had farm fields, but it also had immense patches of woods, not oak and elm but aspen, birch, pine and spruce, jack pine, and tamarack. It was sparsely populated as far as people were concerned, but rich with a diverse population of wildlife. And they, too, were preparing to hide from the approaching menace.

Two and a half hours in the air left the robin bewildered and fatigued to the point of exhaustion. But still the storm was just behind him, pushing him on. And now it was being joined by another enemy, the dark of night.

Weak and worn-out, the robin finally gave up and fluttered down toward the ground. But luck was with him again. Instead of landing in a field or a lake where he surely would have died, he landed in an immense 130-year-old white pine, still standing after hundreds of storms like this.

The robin used his last bit of energy to clasp the branch on which he'd landed. As it swayed violently, he inched toward the trunk of the tree. Then he hopped down in the dark, from branch to branch along the trunk, sheltered from some of the force of the wind, finally getting a secure grip on a small branch that was protected from the wind by the tree trunk. It began to rain and hail, and the storm whipped the pine viciously, but the robin was protected from the worst of it.

So he closed his eyes and with the enduring patience of wild things, snuggled down on his perch, waiting in exhaustion for whatever nature dealt him.

The first part of the evening was fierce as the storm vented its fury on the lightly populated Minnesota northlands. But gradually the wind subsided and the rain turned into a drizzle, then a sprinkle, and then finally stopped altogether.

The wind shifted abruptly and became a gentle breeze from the northwest. As the robin sensed the change, he moved about on his perch slightly and opened his eyes to see pinpoints of light in the blackness above, light that he associated with fair weather. And then he went back to sleep to recover his strength.

At dawn he awoke to a familiar sound, the singing of territorial male robins. He noticed that the robins were more widely dispersed here than in his usual haunts, and there were other sounds that he did not recognize.

He was very hungry, but he did not move. He sat still, partly because of the unfamiliarity of his surroundings but also because he was stiff and sore, especially his breast muscles, which he had strained so much, and the muscles in the lower portion of his body, which controlled his tail.

The young robin sat stiffly for several minutes slowly looking about, taking in the strange features of this new world in which fate had placed him. One thing he noticed was that he was very high up, much higher than he often flew. The big white pine had a "brother" pine about two hundred feet away that was also occupied near the top. And the occupant frightened the young robin.

As pine trees go, it must have once been a beauty. But now the tree was about half dead, and all the uppermost branches were devoid of needles. What would have been the tip of the tree was gone, and in a large fork about as high as the young robin sat was a huge platform of sticks. On top of the platform were a large bird and its two young. The adult bird was black and white and reminded the young robin of the crow that had attacked the nest when he was young. This is not to say that he had a conscious memory of the event, but he did have a fear of all large birds, partly because of the excitement and pain of the crow's attack and also because of his inherited memory. This new large bird had other features that the robin feared—huge talons with long, sharp claws on them and a ferocious-looking hooked beak.

What the robin didn't know and couldn't sense was that this bird, an Osprey, would not consider preying on another bird. Its meal of choice was fish.

Nevertheless, it frightened the young robin so much that he dropped from the branch and dove through the widely spread limbs of the big pine toward the thicker undergrowth of aspen and balsam fir. He flew about thirty yards across the top of the aspen trees and then spotted a clearing. There, sitting on a stump at the edge of the clearing, was another robin, a juvenile about his age. Curious, the young robin landed in a nearby tree just as the other robin glided from the stump to the middle of the clearing, nearly disappearing in the tall grass. The young robin did the same, thinking that perhaps he would find some food there. But instead of flying to the middle of the clearing, he flew to its edge, landing just inside the boundary where the woods ended and the clearing began.

There was a great difference between this place and his regular hunting grounds. Instead of neatly trimmed grass, he found deep, moist piles of leaves. He ran a few feet and paused. Nothing. He repeated the action several times, each time with no success. He couldn't even see dirt, let alone worms. Then something inside him made him turn over a leaf. Instantly a small bug tried to flee, but the robin was too fast and gobbled it right up. So he turned over another leaf. There was an earthworm— a small one, to be sure, but food nonetheless. Soon he was hunting as though he'd been a woodland robin all his life, turning over leaves, looking among the branches of the bushes and tall strands of grass for worms, bugs, and insects. A couple of times he picked up prey that tasted bitter, and he dropped it; he would remember to never again taste anything that looked like it. But most of what he found was excellent fare, and it wasn't long before his stomach was full.

The other juvenile in the middle of the clearing must have had the same success, for suddenly it called out and took flight, darting into the woods and flying low, far beneath the tops of the trees. The young robin pursued his cousin, twisting and weaving through the trunks of aspens and maples, circumventing some pines and balsams, and then heading toward a mass of low shrubs and trees. The other robin landed on a dogwood bush, and the young robin stopped too, landing on a dead branch that stuck out at a right angle from the trunk of a dead aspen tree. He looked down and saw water, a woodland swamp hole that filled up after every shower. He could see several of these sweetwater drinking spots, and ahead lay a larger slough that extended into the bush as far as he could see.

The robin that led him to this delightful spot hopped into the water to drink and bathe, so he did too, accepting again without question the fate that nature had dealt him. For a long while he would remain a woodland robin, out of touch with humans, living like the first robins seen by the settlers of this country, wild, alert, and feeding as much on things at eye level as on those things on and in the earth. It was the start of some pleasant days.

SUMMER

THE YOUNG ROBIN spent his first week as a woodland bird in satisfying and uneventful wandering. He stayed near his juvenile companion most of the time, and they spent their days feeding, bathing, drinking, preening, and just relaxing.

Food was plentiful, and the young robins had a great deal of free time. Between hunts they bathed in woodland pools and then dozed and preened in the branches of the medium-sized aspen and birch trees that were so abundant. Occasionally they were joined for a few hours by another juvenile robin or two, and twice that first week they were driven off by territorial robins protecting their young broods.

But mostly it was a time of rest and relaxation for them. The birds were still growing. Their muscles were developing, their tail feathers were not quite at full length yet, but they were getting stronger every day. It was such a calm time of life that they paid little heed to the direction in which they wandered. They did not seek out any special roosting site but simply slept at night wherever their day's travels left them.

What the young robin did not know was that he and his young companion were heading northeast, at a pace of six to eight miles per day. Wandering is not unusual in young or adult birds. It is one way in which a species tests the limits of its normal habitat. These two were pioneers in a sense, even though other robins had been here before them, as had their ancestors. In fact, robins had been regular residents of these northern woods for thousands of years, coming to repopulate the area after every forest fire and gradually dwindling in numbers as the big pines grew back to sterilize much of the understory (as far as robins were concerned), destroying the varied habitats and fruit-bearing shrubs that robins rely upon for sustenance.

For five weeks the birds flitted on in their unplanned, unregulated, unintentional wandering, following the course laid down by the alternating south and west winds of late summer. This does not mean that they wandered consistently to the northeast. Some days they hardly moved at all. Some days they moved to the east. On others they would go north. And sometimes they would wander to the south and west. But the end result was a gradual movement that led them to a barrier.

And what a barrier!

It was the second week of August. The morning began quietly. There was little singing in the woods at this time of year. Instead, except for the calls of the Pine Siskins and pewees, and the softer twits of the myriad warblers (many of them already into their southward migration), it was still—the kind of quiet monotony typical of the dog days of August.

The two robins, which had roosted on different branches of the same balsam fir, woke up hungry and thirsty. They quickly dropped to the woodland floor below. An old logging trail, now grown over with clover and grasses, it provided a feeding area for several types of wildlife. About a hundred yards down the trail a female Ruffed Grouse and her eight half-grown youngsters were hesitantly walking into the open from their evening roost in a stand of young aspens, so dense that the people who live here call them dog-hair aspens.

The robins hunted toward the grouse. The young thrushes were gathering up the many insects that wandered on the forest floor. The grouse covey, coming from the opposite direction, packed their stomachs with clover leaves and tiny cream-colored mushrooms that sprouted here and there in the shady spots on the trail.

As the birds neared each other, the robin saw the mother grouse's head shoot straight up and heard her cluck to her young. Such a quick movement alerted the young robin to a possible threat.

The grouse became agitated and flicked her wide gray-and-black-striped tail open and shut like a nervous dancer with a fan. And then she suddenly exploded into the air with a loud, rumbling whir. With that, several of her chicks flew too, joining her in the thick alders that grew about ten yards from the trail. But three others, still unaware of the exact nature of the danger, ran into the taller grass at the side of the trail and froze.

At that moment the robins saw the threat, leaped off the ground, and climbed straight up to the branches above. It wasn't a predator. They were afraid of getting trampled to death. An enormous bull moose was rumbling down the trail, his antlers in velvet, his temper short because of the eighty or so deerflies following him, and his speed remarkable.

. . .

He disappeared as quickly as he had arrived. But the robins felt as though they'd had enough to eat and began their daily search for water. A certain playfulness overtook the young male. He pushed off his branch and squealed his flight call at his woodland robin companion. The woodland robin shared his enthusiasm and joined in a combination game of chase and follow the leader. He always maintained a five-yard interval but stayed exactly behind the young robin, duplicating every twist, turn, and drop.

The young robin found this an enjoyable kind of play. Like much of the play of young animals, it had survival value. Twisting to avoid a branch. Climbing suddenly to shoot through an opening between the branches of an aspen tree. Dropping with wings closed for the same reason. Twisting, turning, and keeping a speed of a not-too-demanding twenty-five miles an hour. For five minutes they maintained the game until a sudden change in geography ended it abruptly. The birds found themselves at the top of a cliff. Below, the land fell away rapidly for about two miles. And beyond that stretched a vast expanse of water as far as they could see.

They had stumbled upon Lake Superior.

A splashing noise caused them to look to their left, where they saw a stream that had eroded part of the rock that formed the cliff on which they sat. There was a small falls and a succession of rapids and pools as the stream cut and twisted its way toward the deep depression that formed the bowl of Lake Superior.

Even up on the cliff, the birds sensed the tempering effect of this vast lake on the climate, and they saw evidence of the change—evidence that would mean survival for any bird that ate fruit. Scattered throughout the hills and gently sloping gullies and valleys below were hundreds of mountain ash trees, each loaded with big bunches of red berries just starting to ripen. And throughout the understory spread a variety of berry-laden plants. Blueberries, nannyberries, arrowwood, dogwood, currants, and high-bush cranberries, to name a few. It was truly a fruit-eating bird's paradise, and the bird population of the region substantiated it. For example, they could hear the gentle whispering calls of Cedar Waxwings everywhere. These late-nesting birds time their breeding so that their young leave the nest just as the berries are ripe.

And as the young robins soon found out, many robins made this area home as well. Thirsty from their flight, the two young birds flew over the cliff but immediately felt insecure at being exposed at such a height. In response, they alternately closed and opened their wings to lose altitude until they once again resumed normal flight just over the tops of the trees that grew along the lakeshore. They flew to the river that shone so brightly from the sky and then landed on a group of three-foot-high boulders that jutted out of the water in the middle of the river just before it emptied into the lake.

There the swiftly flowing water was caught in numerous rocks and twisted into shallow eddies just right for bathing and quenching their thirst. The young robin went through his bathing ritual and then flew to a branch on one of the thousands of birch trees that grew throughout the area. However, his woodland companion did not follow him. Instead he flew to the other side of the river to preen. The young robin never saw his friend again. Such is the way of wild things. Friendships, if they can be called such, are fleeting. The suburban robin was following his drives, and the woodland robin his. For a while those drives happened to coincide. Now they did not, so the birds went their separate ways with no feelings of loss or loneliness, no feelings of despair—in fact no feelings at all. Each was too busy satisfying his own needs. And each was secure in his inherited knowledge that others of the same species were everywhere.

After ten minutes of preening, the young robin flew across the river, again in a northeasterly direction, to a bush that was loaded with dark blue fruit. He had never eaten a nannyberry before, but it looked good to him. Besides that, in a larger bush about forty feet away he saw three other robins, each poking and pulling at the individual berries on its branches.

The young robin hopped down several branches until he came to the tip of one that had a good number of berries on it. The branch was bent toward the ground, and his weight made it hang down even farther. It was hard to get a grip on it, and he had to flutter while trying to pick off a berry. But finally he got one firmly in his bill and pulled it away from the stem. Quickly he forced it down, then pulled off another and another. After five berries he stopped, for he felt very full and satisfied. He was thirsty again, so he flew back to the river, where he drank the cold, clear water, enjoying it as he raised his head to let each beakful flow down his throat. Then he flew across the river again, just opposite the nannyberry where he had seen the other robins.

There was little wind, but the constant gurgling of the rapidly moving water drowned out the usual background noises of the forest. It made it impossible to hear the droning buzz of the many insects that were so thick in the woods at this time of year. The young robin could not hear many bird sounds either, yet the sound of the water pleased him and dulled his senses, combining with the fullness of his stomach to make him drowsy.

He closed his eyes and napped. But about three minutes later he was startled awake. Something had happened, but he didn't know what. He sensed that something was wrong and instinctively froze, except for his eyes. He looked across the river toward a mountain ash tree and thought he could see the motionless silhouettes of a pair of robins. But they weren't moving either. His instinct was to join them. However, since they were still except for occasional slight head movements, he felt safest staying where he was. Just then, one of the silhouettes suddenly moved its head, and as the young robin was about to push off his perch to join it he saw a blurred shape flying over the river from his left toward the bird that had just moved. The robin remained still, petrified with fear. The blur took form in his eyes as a medium-sized, long-tailed bird flew extremely fast toward the robin that had moved, a juvenile about his age. Too late the targeted robin tried to flee. In a puff of feathers he was hit and fell limply to the ground, followed by the hawk. The other robins in the tree scattered into the woods, but the hawk, a small falcon called a Merlin that specializes in preying on birds, paid no attention to them. The Merlin had made its kill, and now it dropped to the ground to slice the skin from the robin's breast and pull off strips of dark red meat with its sharp hooked bill.

The young robin turned to flee to the cover of the woods. His basic lesson of survival was once again reinforced. Here, as everywhere, there were creatures that would eat him. He had to be alert at all times.

He stayed in the woods but flew parallel to the Lake Superior shoreline. About a hundred yards from the mouth of the river, he stopped abruptly, landing in a gnarled old birch tree that was half dead and bent over from the abuse of the cold wind, icy winter spray, and storms from the lake.

To the west the sun was sinking slowly. The robin rested for a few seconds. He didn't appreciate the beauty of the scene—sunsets and sunrises were simply events in his life—but he did feel a kind of peace. He felt, in spite of the Merlin attack he had just witnessed, good in this place.

And except for an occasional fright from a predator, the next few weeks would be good. He needed plenty of food and a minimum of stress to build up his strength, because soon he would face another journey, the longest of his life.

He flitted a few feet into a small cedar tree, hopped close to the trunk, and tucked his bill under his left wing. All he could hear as he fell asleep was the constant rhythmic sound of Lake Superior's surf upon the rocky beach. The plentiful days of summer would soon be over.

10

FALL

H E WAS CHANGING slightly every day, though the changes were not readily apparent to an observer. He was becoming stronger, even more alert, and at times he showed a kind of friendly abrasiveness to other robins he would come across. He liked to challenge them and chase them, though sometimes he would be chased as well. He was also changing in another way that made him feel uncomfortable. Daily, feathers were being replaced all over his body as he shed his juvenile plumage for the moderate brown, black, and reddish orange that would mark him as a fall adult. Many feathers had white tips, and the colors would not be as bright and bold as the breeding colors he would wear next spring (if he survived), but they marked him as already being a survivor. Since growing the new feathers made him feel uncomfortable, he devoted much time each day to preening and scratching. As new feathers worked their way from beneath the skin, old feathers became loose, creating considerable itching. And the only way to fix the itch was to scratch it, a chore at which most birds are remarkably adept.

They have the right tools—a beak that's made for prying and poking and an amazingly flexible musculoskeletal system that lets them deliver the bill or the foot to the itch, no matter where on their body the itch is.

At all times of the year, but especially during the molt, scratching, itching, preening, and oiling of the feathers are important robin activities. Throughout August and into September, adult birds replace feathers worn from their hard summer of feeding and raising young. The young birds, at the same time, develop their first winter plumage, shedding their juvenile garb and growing an extra layer of down and feathers in preparation for the cold season ahead, but keeping their wing and tail feathers. Adult robins replace their wing and tail feathers, worn from the strain of nesting. And all robins eat to build up fat stores, the energy for the long flights they will make to their winter ranges.

So it was that the young robin spent great portions of each day working on his body, pulling feathers, massaging his skin with his bill, scratching the base of his wing joints with his feet, going over and over every bit of his body.

Since it was a season of plenty, all the robins had considerable time to devote to their molt. With mountain ash, dogwood berries, and high-bush cranberries available, there was more than enough food to go around for both the robins and the hordes of Cedar Waxwings that were starting to wander in family groups through the northern forest.

Some years, because of inappropriate weather conditions, this wasn't the case. If there was a shortage of berries, the robins would eat more insect matter and wander far and wide in search of food. But in this year's abundance the birds took advantage of their opportunities and became almost exclusively eaters of wild fruit, only occasionally supplementing their diet with insect fare.

In addition to his changing appearance (the spotted breast was going), the young robin was experiencing a transformation in his behavior. He felt a strong need to be near other robins. Each day this drive became more intense, until finally he found his actions more or less governed by the behavior of the other birds around him.

He was also testing his strength. That is, he would try to dominate birds that he recognized as being smaller and more submissive than himself, chasing them or just confronting them so they would yield to his space, or his claim of a branch or a berry. He also found himself yielding to other, larger birds, usually adult males who had already lived through one or more breeding seasons.

As a result of these changes, he found that he had become a member of a small flock ranging in size from ten to twenty birds. The number in the flock varied nearly every day, as some birds would drop out to travel with other flocks and others would join in. The survival value of the loose-knit organization was obvious. Ten pairs of eyes were more likely to spot danger than one pair, and ten pairs of eyes could cover more territory in the roving hunt for food and fruit trees. A flock of birds also gave the individual a greater opportunity to avoid predators. That is, a single bird in a flock of ten has only a 10 percent chance of being the target of an air or ground predator—compared to a 100 percent chance for a lone bird that is spotted by a predator.

Throughout early September the flock roamed up and down the Minnesota shore of Lake Superior, staying within five to ten miles of the lake—and usually a lot closer than that.

. . .

Twice in the middle of the month the flock was attacked by raptors, once by a Merlin and once by a much slower Broad-winged Hawk. Each time the members escaped. One bird was taken at night by an Eastern Screech-Owl, but for the most part the days and nights were uneventful. During this period the sky overhead was filled with hawks; they funneled along the shore of Lake Superior because of their dislike for flying over the water and because of the favorable air currents where the land rose from the lake.

The young robin was almost an adult bird now. He was still sexually immature, but he had discarded his juvenile plumage. As robins go he was quite typical. He was a large, healthy male but certainly not the dominant bird in any flock. In fact, he took a place nearer the bottom of the hierarchy because larger, faster adult birds, both male and female, dominated the top. But that was good for him because they seemed to have greater certainty in their actions and reactions to the environment around him as a result of their experience. It was good for him to follow and learn.

By the last week in September, frost had already killed the softer plants and kissed the leaves with touches of yellow and crimson on the higher ground away from the lake. With the frost and the falling of the leaves, robins appeared to be having even more of a good time. Less of the day was devoted to preening and more to flying, chasing, and even singing—soft snippets of song. When the whole flock was loafing in the trees, calling and singing, it was quite a musical event. At night the birds would seek out thick growth in swampy areas and would very quietly sneak into roosting spots, as furtive and stealthy as any woodland thrush.

But they became increasingly restless during the day. By mid-October the young robin could feel within himself a combination of energy and a sense of belonging, of being a social member of a flock. It was as if the society of robins was the only thing that mattered at this time of the year. Typically, a day would go like this:

With dawn he would wake and sit on his branch, ready for flight but awaiting the lead from older birds in his flock. He would be alerted before the flight by a couple of quiet, low calls exchanged by several of the robins. Then the flock would follow two or three of the most dominant birds, climbing to just above the treetops for the flight out of the roosting grounds. Usually that flight lasted at most only three or four minutes. Silently the robins would descend on an area filled with mountain ash trees or dogwood bushes. Then the birds would eat, calling occasionally in the predawn grayness but remaining mostly quiet. After feeding, the flock would depart in a scattered fashion (always leaving a few birds behind but always picking others up as they flew). They would then rise to just above the highest trees, flying to the nearest water source to drink and bathe.

On this day, the watering area was about forty yards down a hill from an extensive woods filled with mature, heavily fruited mountain ash trees, an ideal situation for the robins. All day long the birds alternately fed and watered themselves, dozing occasionally and chasing each other frequently in mock battles to test dominance and build muscle strength.

As the sun climbed, the birds became bolder and louder in their activities and calls. Also, as the sun reached down to the forest floor, some of the robins would land in open areas, snapping up insects to add protein and fat to their diet.

Before night fell, the birds retired again to a swampy area and became quiet, furtive, silent, protecting themselves from attack by owls and other night predators. Each day more leaves fell, and each day the birds felt increasingly restless. But the abundant berries kept them from wandering very far. As long as food and water were available, the robins were inclined to stay. In fact, it was not uncommon for robins to be seen in this far north country throughout the winter. Lake Superior tempers the climate until the ice extends far from shore, and in many winters its feeding streams and brooks provide ample water for the robins to enjoy throughout the winter. And in years when the berries are as abundant as they were this year, some robins stay near the food supply and winter over quite successfully. The cold doesn't present a major problem as long as there is enough food and water.

Nevertheless, gradually the number of robins along the shore dwindled, leaving the vast quantities of berries for the still present Cedar Waxwings and perhaps an influx of Bohemian Waxwings during the winter.

The restlessness that caused so many robins to move out—and that was so much a part of most bird life—gained control of the young robin and his flock one morning too. He sensed the change in the wind from east to north at night, and it caused him to wake up, as it did several of the birds in the roost area. One bird called and others answered, but they did not move. However, as dawn began to lighten the sky, the dominant older birds in the flock called out, a different call than the ones the young robin had heard before, and they rose from the branches, climbing first to treetop level and then even higher as the last birds in the flock caught up.

One young male rose with the others to treetop height, but then, as the older birds led the way even higher in a gradual, energy-saving climb, he dropped back down to the forest. For some reason, it just wasn't his time to migrate, though he would eventually do so, with a different flock a couple of weeks later.

The young robin was exhilarated. The climb was taking him higher than he had ever been in his life. Oh, how comfortable it was. The total sensation of it all—other birds calling back and forth, being with the other robins, seeing their wings flash with every stroke, hearing the air rush past and being pushed by his wings, seeing the tail feathers of the birds ahead open and close slightly, exposing the little white patches at the outermost feathers of each robin's tail, all together in a loose group, heading southwest. Most of all, he felt powerful and confident as they rose to this new altitude.

He felt a part of the whole, and he had a sense of security in this group that he had never felt when he was alone. He felt that the group knew where it was going—in fact, there was no doubt that the group did—though the young robin himself did not know at all where they were headed. But he did have a feeling, a sense of where to go. It felt right.

Slowly they continued their climb, and the pointed tops of the balsams and jack pines below got smaller and smaller. To his left there was water as far as he could see. To his right was the forest, now half naked but red, orange, brown, and gray, with dozens of lakes pocking the terrain. Below stood the cliffs, rocks, and trees that marked the edge of the great depression that formed Lake Superior.

The flock was using the boundary of the lake as a navigational aid. They were flying about a mile from the lake, keeping themselves in an air layer above the somewhat warmer air tempered by the forty-five-degree lake water. Their climb became even more gradual as they found a favorable air current, and they finally stopped climbing at about eight hundred feet, where they were getting a nice assist from a fifty-mile-an-hour breeze from the north.

The flight of the flock was rapid, but easygoing and comfortable. The birds were scattered over about forty yards and were formed in what can only be described as a bunch. They had neither the aerodynamic grace of a V-shaped formation of Canada Geese nor the wheeling symmetry of a flock of shorebirds or diving ducks. Instead, it was like a gathering of good friends who happened to be going to the same place at the same time. The young robin held a position at the left-hand side of this group and felt little fatigue as the birds progressed. After about two hours in the air, he could see changes taking place in the land. To his left, across the water, he could now detect land, which gradually got closer. And after forty more minutes of cruising, he could see far ahead that the lake ended.

As the flock got closer to this termination point, he noticed familiar sights: roofs, houses, streets, chimneys, crisscrossing patterns of streets and alleys, things that he knew and was familiar with, things that several of the juveniles in this flock had never seen.

Slowly the birds approached the large city that was on this end of the lake, and they felt reluctant to continue on. The lake had been their abundant and primary source of water for so many weeks that they didn't want to leave it.

Their reluctance was combined with great thirst and a desire to bathe that was unanimous throughout the flock. One of the older birds gave a "follow me" call and began to descend rapidly toward the edge of the city below. He was an experienced migrant and had once landed in the concrete and brick downtown area of a large city. He didn't want to do that again. He did not actually remember the incident, but he did have a fear of concentrations of large structures. Thus he led the flock in a steep descent toward the suburbs of this large city. There he knew he would find the habitat that he required. The others would profit by his experience, and they would all be able to stay near the lake.

Calling excitedly, the birds closed their wings, dropped twenty or thirty feet, and then opened their wings to brake their fall, to stay within a safe (meaning comfortable) airspeed. In about thirty seconds they had descended to treetop height, and the lead birds stopped for a few seconds to rest their tired breast muscles while the slower birds arrived.

Then abruptly they were off again, shooting through the treetops as they sought the lakeshore. They flew over a couple of streets, dipped down to cruise over the lawn and grounds of a lakeshore mansion, then rose again over the buildings to reach the lake. Where the estate grounds joined the lake they found what they were looking for—pools in the rocks where the waves had splashed over. Pools of cold, clear water from which to drink and in which to bathe.

The young robin stuck his bill into a small pool barely larger than he was, filled his lower beak with water, and then raised his head to let the water flow down his throat. It was good. He repeated that five more times and then jumped into the pool. His splashing made a little rainbow in the bright October sunshine as he soaked his feathers. Then he spent several minutes on the rocks, preening and rearranging his feathers, before flying to a shrubbery bed that edged the grounds of the estate. From a juniper tree he pulled five large berries, and found a couple of angleworms and some bugs in a brief hunt on the estate lawn.

He spent the rest of the day eating, drinking, bathing, and sleeping on the estate grounds. As his energy stores rebuilt, he felt the urge coming back, the urge to push on, to be with other robins, the urge to climb high and fly toward the sun. But he and his friends didn't go anywhere that day. When night came, they flew to different protected spots on the estate grounds and fell into a deep sleep. Tomorrow their journey would begin again.

FALL

DAWN. AGAIN HE FELT the drive that had awakened him several times during the night, the deep urge to fly high toward the descending arc of the sun. The urge to go somewhere he had never been but that he somehow knew existed. As before, a few calls were exchanged between birds, and then the flock climbed above the trees in the half-light between night and day. Again the older birds led the way as the small flock climbed high to clear the chimneys and buildings that stood in their way in the distance.

Below, the city stretched out to his right, with the lake to the left. Ore boats and oceangoing freighters were at berths in the harbor, and one long boat loaded with ore was passing beneath a bridge that linked the city with a jutting point of sand that intruded into the lake. Farther to his right were the hills that framed the city. Gradually the robins climbed higher than the hills and saw woodlands speckled with lakes stretching to the horizon.

The city was quiet, unaware of the passage of this small band of wild creatures. But early that October morning a man would comment to his wife that he hadn't seen many robins lately and that perhaps winter was just around the corner.

The robins climbed higher, still flying in a southwesterly direction as they left the city and its checkerboard pattern of streets and buildings. For the first time in their lives several of the birds in the flock were leaving the lake, today in a gray sky with low clouds scudding in from offshore. But they left it without remorse, without a thought about what was behind them. They did not know remorse or melancholy. They were concerned only with now and what lay ahead.

Many of the leaves were off the trees, and the forest floor was somewhat exposed. The land ahead of them looked vast, while behind them they could see the familiar lake and its shore. They maintained their southwesterly direction both by the feel for what was right and by the leadership of adult birds, who recognized visual clues such as prominent rivers and lakes. Their innate sensitivity to light made them aware of the shorter days and the apparent movement of the sun to the south along its track in the sky. At this time of year their bodies told them to follow the direction that the sun had taken, to fly toward the space beyond to where the sun was moving.

At one point about fifty minutes from the city, a string of Rusty Blackbirds passed below the robins, their courses intersecting only because the blackbirds were flying due south as the band of robins took a northeast-southwest direction. Elsewhere in the sky the young robin could make out other migrants too. About half a mile to the west he saw another flock of robins flying in about the same direction at the same speed.

And at another point he heard the clamor of a large flock of Canada Geese, their calls noisier than the occasional calls the robins made and the soft sounds of the air being pushed by his wings and rushing past his body. More than fifty geese were flying from the northwest to the southeast at almost the same altitude as the robins. At first the size of these birds frightened the young robin, but when the older birds in the robins' flock did not show signs of fear he took a good look at the gray-and-white birds flying in a loose V-shaped formation.

Even ten minutes after their paths had crossed he could still detect them because of their huge size. But gradually the more rapidly moving geese faded into the fuzziness beyond sight and continued their flight toward the fields in southern Illinois where their ancestors had been wintering for centuries.

Below, after two hours and nearly eighty miles (thanks to the push of the northerly winds), the character of the land gradually began to change. There were more square fields and areas where the forest was yielding to meadow and cropland. Oaks and maples became more abundant, replacing pine and fir on the south-facing slopes, including some wide-spreading red oaks, tenaciously holding on to their faded leaves as if unwilling to admit that winter was on the way and that life would soon come to a standstill for the plants of the forest.

Small towns became more common, too, as the vastness of the northern forest faded behind the flock. The young robin saw the familiar sight of big round water towers jutting above many of the villages—problems, perhaps, for migrating birds that flew at night closer to the ground.

Several miles to the right of the flock was a lake, fully as large as that part of Lake Superior near the estate where they had spent the evening. And about half an hour after passing that, they saw the first signs of a large city, to the left of their course. To the robin leading this small bunch, each major landmark was familiar, something he recalled from his memory, a point that told him in what direction he should fly, a point that reinforced his inner feeling to fly toward the sun.

To the youngest robin, and the other two juveniles in the flock, these landmarks were permanently etched in their memories. Recognition of them could have survival value at another time, for landmarks have always provided cues for birds that migrate in daylight. Of course, landmarks are also visible at night in good weather conditions, and it is no coincidence that obliteration of landmarks by fog and storms causes many disasters and unpleasant incidents for migrating birds.

There were other factors at work, of course. Robins didn't migrate just by tradition. They had a feeling, a drive that pushed them toward a certain direction. But for many that would return to the area where they learned to fly, tradition was an important means of finding adequate viable habitat.

The great hazy structure that was the city grew larger and stretched farther across the horizon as the flock got closer to it. And as they turned slightly to the west to avoid a cloudy reddish haze that seemed to hang over the city, they saw another significant landmark looming on the horizon— another lake, with a wandering, irregular shoreline.

To the young robin this seemed very familiar. The landmarks were important to him and invaded his consciousness with an instant familiarity. Indeed, as they flew across a bay of the lake at treetop height and he looked to the south and west, he could make out the chimney, the most important landmark from his first days alone. Seeing it did not overwhelm him. His instinct to stay with other robins was stronger than the recollections of his wandering days and nights at the roost, so he remained with his peers, landing finally on the southerly side of a large bay of the lake amid some small homes and tangles of sumac bushes. Two and three at a time, the robins drank from the cool lake while the others sat in nearby trees, each twenty or thirty feet from the others.

After the birds finished watering and preening, they flew to the sumac thicket and adjoining lawns. They were weary from their four-hour, 150-mile flight, and their bodies needed rest and replenishment. Each robin knew that soon the flock would be on the way again, pushing toward the sun.

After the young robin ate a couple of sumac berries, he flew toward one of the houses, attracted by the gleam on a bush near a corner of the house. Several large white berries hung there, each about the size of a marble. Some were beginning to turn brown and wither, but most were pure white and looked appetizing. He fluttered to the bush and tried to pull one off while hovering but was unsuccessful. So he hopped and flew up to the bush again. Finally, after much flapping of wings, he was able to grasp one of the twiggy little branches firmly. It bent considerably under his weight, but he managed to gulp down two of the white berries before relinquishing his position to gravity.

His activities attracted a couple of older robins, so he gave up his position to them and hunted around toward the back of the cottage. On the lawn by its back door was a small band of House Sparrows eating pieces of bread that had been thrown on the lawn. The young robin had never eaten bread before, but it was white, like the berries he had eaten, and it was being consumed by the other birds. He ran over to a piece of it, frightening off the smaller male sparrow, who hopped out of pecking range but remained nearby, reluctant to leave his prize.

The robin took the piece of bread in his beak and shook it until the part in his beak broke off from the rest. Then he swallowed it. It felt and tasted good to him, so he took another piece, and another. But the dryness of the bread made him thirsty, so he flew away from the sparrows, turned the corner of the house, and headed to the lakefront beyond the cottage. There he took several deep drinks from a sheltered puddle on the beach. Next he flew to the sumac bush to sit and preen and in a few minutes found himself alternately dozing and preening as the meal in his stomach digested.

So it went for the entire flock the rest of that week—feeding, resting, preening, drinking and bathing, working hard to build up their strength.

After a week the temperature chilled overnight. As the birds slept among the cattails at the mouth of a creek that flowed out of the bay, they could feel the wind pick up from the southeast, accompanied by a steady cooling. It was damp, too, and slowly a warm drizzle began to spatter off the backs of the robins.

The young male was awakened by the change in the weather and fluffed up his feathers. He was afraid to move in the dark but did not want to remain where he was. So he sat there, awake, alert, and somewhat uncomfortable as the drizzle fell upon him, waiting with the patience that birds know best. The patience that lets the mother owl sit on her nest for weeks. The patience that lets the Ruffed Grouse spend its winter days in a snowbank, leaving only to eat the buds of aspen trees. Waiting for light that means safety.

About a foot below him a muskrat pushed through the cattails in the dark on an urgent mission to gather more materials to pack his house higher before the ice set in.

In the distance he heard the low hoot of a Barred Owl, and he heard screaming and whining from the shore near the mouth of the creek as two young raccoons fought over possession of a crawfish, oblivious to the drizzle in their evening frenzy to fill their gullets. They were fat from feasting on frogs rushing to hibernate in the muddy lake bottom, but now most of the amphibians were in the water and the hunt for food was becoming more difficult each night.

Finally the sky lightened and the young robin left his perch in the rushes. Though he heard the other robins call, he flew back to the cottage instead of joining them. But the snowberries were all gone. He went to the lawn and ran up and down. He picked up a few small bugs, but not nearly enough to sate the hunger within him. Then he remembered the bread. He flew to the back door of the cottage where there had been bread all week, but today there was none.

Puzzled and hungry, the young robin suddenly sensed his aloneness and felt a need to be near the others of his flock. He flew up to the cottage roof. He looked for the other robins but could not see them anywhere. He called out, but there was no answer. In his haste and hunger, his drive to replenish himself, he had been left behind by his traveling companions. With the light they had flown on. Already they were miles beyond him, flying at treetop height in the mist toward the south.

The young robin's impulses had him confused. He was hungry and fatigued. He felt a need to be with other robins. And he felt that urge to fly in the direction of the sun.

Finally the drive to migrate overcame all the rest and he took off through the trees, flying toward the sun but looking always for fruit-bearing trees or bushes. Although he was on his own he still kept to the same course, flying to the southwest, slightly away from the rain and drizzle that was now moving a little more easterly every few minutes.

Once, to avoid flying through a particularly dense maple, he rose above the treetops and saw again the chimney that had been so important to him early in his life. Now, afraid, alone, hungry, and full of the ominous feeling of danger, he changed course and flew toward the landmark as if it would guide him to the security of those carefree days.

When he was almost there, suddenly he was no longer flying in drizzle. The wind had shifted even farther from the east and the drizzle had become a damp, wet snow that nearly obliterated his view of the brick chimney. Finally, he was near it, and there he saw the great expanse of lawn that had been his hunting ground so long ago. He was pleased to see the thick hedge of barberry and the dense blue spruce trees, for they looked secure to him in this threatening weather. He descended rapidly, landing near the middle of the lawn.

Several quick runs across the lawn yielded nothing to eat, and the ever-thickening snowfall made him feel even more insecure. Again he ran along the ground, pausing and looking for some activity. Each pause was without reward. Once he saw something that might have been a dead bug, so he reached to pick it up. But it was a pebble and he quickly dropped it.

The snow intensified, and some of the flakes were beginning to accumulate on the ground, causing great anxiety for the young robin. He had never seen snow before and he didn't like it. He flew a short distance from the lawn to a sidewalk that remained free of snow even though it was beginning to cover the grass. Next to the sidewalk grew a three-foot-high barberry hedge with sharp thorns on the branches. There, dangling from the ends of hundreds of the branches, were teardrop-shaped red fruits. The robin had never tried anything like this before, but the fruit looked good and the color was similar to that of other berries he had enjoyed in the past.

He fluttered up and grabbed a berry in his beak. Back on the ground he opened his mouth wide and swallowed the berry. It felt good to him, and in a few minutes he had consumed six of the berries. Finally, his stomach could hold no more, so he left the ground and flew into one of the spruce trees that grew along the west wall of a three-story administration building, an area well protected from the wind and snow now blowing directly from the east.

He spent most of the rest of the day in that spruce, leaving to drink from puddles in the street and on the sidewalk and to eat the barberry fruits. For the most part he sat patiently in the tree, building his strength and waiting out the storm, which steadily increased in intensity. By four o'clock that afternoon the robin felt most comfortable not moving. So he stayed on his branch as the wind howled and the storm raged. And when it got dark, he closed his eyes and slept soundly.

By two o'clock the following morning, the wind had shifted to the northwest, the sky had cleared, and four inches of wet, slushy snow had accumulated on the ground near the Twin Cities region of Minnesota. Farther south, near Mankato, a freezing rain had caused numerous traffic accidents throughout the day. In one, a small band of robins had landed, confused, in the middle of a busy access road to Highway 169. A motorist swerved to avoid the birds and drove her car into the ditch, cracking her collarbone and dislocating her knee.

Two highway patrolmen on the scene verified her story. They had seen eight robins, still standing near the shoulder of the road. It appeared as though ice and snow had accumulated on their wings and backs and they were too heavy to fly.

The fate of the birds was not determined.

12

FALL

I T WAS COLD WHEN the robin woke up, and his sense of the cold, the wind, and his urge to fly with it made him eager to leave. It was as if the wind was blowing to help him because of the strength of the rush of air at twenty miles an hour, gusting to forty, and because of its direction from the northwest.

In addition, he was nervous because of the new appearance of his world—snow blanketed the ground and clung to the trees and bushes. It had covered up his hunting spots, and he sensed immediately that it would be difficult to find food.

A loud roaring sound broke the morning stillness. To his left the robin saw a man thing pushing a large red object that threw snow high into the air. As the man moved this noisy object, the robin saw that the hard area next to the barberry hedge was no longer covered with snow. It was the sidewalk, and the robin knew that it did not contain food. Yet he felt a need to fly to it and walk on it. He left his limb on the spruce, knocking a couple of puffs of snow loose, and glided down to the sidewalk, landing about five feet behind the man and the noisy machine.

To his right were the bushes and to his left was the snow, even higher than he was, a discomforting sight. The robin fluttered up into the bushes and landed on one frail branch that drooped down into the snow as he tried in vain to reach a berry. But his balance was not good, so from there he fluttered to a sturdier branch and gobbled up four berries.

With his appetite somewhat sated, the uncomfortable nervous feeling returned. He flew to the cleared part of the sidewalk, shivered all over, and fluffed his feathers in response to the chill he felt.

He looked at the man with the machine, still blowing snow high into the air. Then he glanced back at the bush and the bare sidewalk. It was almost as if he decided: "This is enough of this. I'm leaving." He leaped into the air, called out as if hoping that another robin would answer, and flew toward the man. But the man never heard the young robin over the roar of his snow blower and thus never saw the bird as it passed overhead and began climbing higher than the treetops.

Obeying his feelings, the young robin flew using the wind for assistance as he aimed south-southwest. His direction was no conscious navigation, just a feeling that it was the proper direction in which to go.

The naked, snow-covered branches, waving not nearly as gracefully without leaves as they did when they had leaves, gave in stiffly to the force of the wind. The young robin looked from horizon to horizon for others of his kind, but he saw only an occasional crow or Blue Jay cruising just above the treetops in search of food, mischief, or both. He could feel the wind's assist and observed it too in the speed at which he flew. He was crossing the earth at between forty and forty-five miles an hour in a flight that seemed effortless to him, except he had to work to maintain his course and deal with frequent wind gusts that disrupted his aerodynamics.

Higher he climbed, finally reaching about five hundred feet. He could see for miles, and he noticed the striking contrast between frozen ponds, which looked like white globs, and the mottled appearance of the rest of the earth, freckled and streaked because of the brush, trees, and stubble sticking up out of the snow. As he flew he continuously looked for others of his kind, but he saw none. Once, off to his left and quite a bit lower, he saw a long string of Red-winged Blackbirds flying south, perhaps three hundred of them, stretched out over a hundred yards or more. But in the aftermath of the storm the skies were mostly vacant.

He flew over woodlands, open creeks, fields and houses, barns, and shelterbelts with evergreens offering a promise of protection and maybe food. But the young robin gave in to the wind and his urge and pushed on to the south-southwest, letting the wind do much of the work, following his ancestors to warmth, food, and survival.

For five long hours he maintained his course. The whiteness beneath him became increasingly scattered until it finally disappeared altogether, giving way to gray earth and faded stalks of corn not yet plowed under. About two miles ahead was a small town, and to the right of it he saw open water, tall spruce trees, and a large area of cattails. After five hours, even though the wind had done much of the work, he needed nourishment and water—most especially water.

The young robin changed direction slightly and passed over a four-lane highway to follow the winding, grassy bed of a dry creek that led to water in the distance. As he flew above the creek and the thickets of cottonwoods, willows, and alders that grew along it, he gradually dropped to fly just above and through the tops of the tallest trees. Finally, with the water in sight, he stopped to rest on the branch of a willow. As he stopped, he felt the fatigue of his journey. But he had a feeling of comfort and security here, without the snow, and he felt more confidence in his ability to find food.

He rested for just a couple of seconds and then pushed off again, flying slowly through the tops of the trees toward water. The creek ran into a large pond. The point at which it entered the pond was a ten-acre area thickly overgrown with cattails. On the far side of the pond, water lapped on a shore that was mostly neatly trimmed and landscaped lawn. Down the shore from the cattails, and between them and the lawn, stood a dense, shrubby thicket.

The young robin flew first to the far side and landed on the lawn next to the water. He ran down to the water and dipped his lower bill into it. He lifted his head high and let the cold, clear liquid flow soothingly down his throat. It felt good, so he drank again and again, taking five deep swallows of water before his thirst was quenched.

Then he felt hungry. He flew across the lake toward the thicket, calling once, thinking that perhaps there might be other robins nearby. But there was no answer.

He flew about ten yards into the thicket before landing to look for signs of fruit or anything else that might be edible. He saw nothing. He flew another ten yards and looked. Nothing. He repeated his search until he finally emerged from the thicket as it ended near a corner of a fenced pasture where several black-and-white cows were grazing. Before venturing among them to search for insects, he landed on the fence, just at the corner near the thicket. He cocked his head to one side, looked down, and saw something. Berries! They were a withered, deep-blue berry of a type that he had not consumed before, but they looked good to him, so he hopped down to the lowest wire of the fence. The berries were scattered along a vine that grew from the end of the thicket and stretched out for several yards along the lower strand of wire. He ate one. It was satisfying. He hopped along the fence, eating each berry as he came to it, often falling nearly upside down as he stretched and fluttered to reach the weather-beaten fruit.

In a few minutes his stomach could hold no more. Satiated, he looked back at the thicket and flew from the fence, steering toward a dense hawthorn bush. He landed on a thorny branch at the outside of the bush and then hopped into the last few branches, finally finding a place that seemed secure and protected on all sides. Then he preened and loafed away the rest of the afternoon, occasionally going back for more berries.

He stayed near the thicket for two days, eating berries, even an occasional weed seed and an insect or two that he found in the pasture. But the nights were cold, and the urge to move on intensified as his strength returned.

On the morning of the third day, after eating a few berries, he flew out of the thicket and over the pond toward the south-southwest. Twice he called his robin flock call, but there was no answer. He paused on the far side of the pond to drink. And though he felt that this might be a good place to stay, his urge to migrate was strong. After a few sips, he flew up to the barren branches of a willow tree that grew near the water. He sat for nearly a minute, then off he flew, twisting and turning through the branches of the willow and the silver maple that grew next to it, breaking through the maze into the sky.

Again he called out, but he was still alone. The sky was overcast and at first there was little wind to either help or hinder him. So he climbed to about three times the height of the trees and settled into a comfortable course with a speed of about thirty miles per hour.

The square fields of Iowa passed beneath him and he saw roads, barns and houses with woodland pastures, occasional thickets near wetlands and creeks, and groves of trees on land that was too steep or sandy to be plowed. Gradually the terrain changed. Hills became more frequent, with more woodlots and thickets.

Once, while passing over a small thicket, he saw three robins flying far below him at a right angle to his flight. He called to them. One of the birds answered, but they continued on their way and he on his, answering different urges, responding to different internal and external stimuli.

Again his flight ended after nearly five hours, and he spent three days near a small pastured woodlot with thickets and a stock pond. He ate mostly hawthorn berries, supplemented by dead insects and pupae that he found underneath fallen leaves.

Again the urge to fly overwhelmed his need for security and protection, and he flew away from the thicket, up and over the hills of southwestern

Iowa, and across the muddy, looping Missouri River, finally landing in a cottonwood grove on the western bank of the Missouri, on the southeastern edge of the state of Nebraska. Again he was tired, but he knew his journey was not yet over, that this wasn't quite the right place to settle in. What he didn't know was that the wind would again have a hand in his fate.

13

FALL

T HE YOUNG ROBIN spent a restless night. The barometric pressure was falling, and like all birds, he was sensitive to the pressure changes, partly because of his relationship to the air as one component of his environment and partly because his bones were hollow and he felt different when his internal pressure was out of whack with what was going on in the air around him.

Besides that, he was awakened several times by upsetting noises. Twice, large flocks of geese flew just overhead, following the course of the Missouri. And throughout the night a Great Horned Owl called out, announcing the boundaries of its hunting territory. The owl's call frightened the robin.

When dawn finally broke, it was more red than usual and the sky threatened a change in the weather. The robin awoke, still fatigued but feeling the need to move on. First he had to drink.

He pushed off from his perch and called out as he flew from the branch. But no other robin answered. He dropped through the branches of the cottonwood tree and leveled off into a long glide to a small backwater that looked shallow. He landed in a tree, looked around, and then glided to a muddy little hump that rose about five inches out of the water.

After landing, he looked again in several directions and then, satisfied that no predators were nearby, dipped his bill into the water and lifted it to drink. Even though the water was somewhat muddy, it was a good feeling, so he took another drink. But just as he rose up, he caught sight of a large shape rushing toward him from his left. Without thinking about what it was, he pushed his feet into the mud and leaped up, flapping his wings with all his strength to flee the threat. It was the owl, in a silent, diving attack on the robin.

The robin cut sharply to the owl's left just as the bird of prey extended his X-shaped claws to snare his victim. The owl tried desperately to make the last-second change in his course that would allow him to grasp the robin. He dropped his left wing to bring his body over while at the same time thrusting his left foot, swinging his tail to the right, and bringing the primary feathers of his right wing straight up. But he missed the robin by three inches, and the momentum of his maneuver forced his left wing to hit the mud, causing him to tumble. The robin fled, scolding.

The attack ended with the wet owl, muddy wing and all, standing half-soaked in water three-fourths of the way up his legs.

The robin, terrified, swerved and dodged through the understory for a full minute before he realized that the owl was no longer after him. After he had rested for a couple of minutes, his feelings returned to normal and the terror of the attack and its memory left the bird's consciousness. But again the lesson was reinforced. Be alert. Always.

The young robin was hungry and desperate to move on to more comfortable surroundings. But he felt a certain anxiety because of the weather. The sun was disappearing under a thickening layer of low gray clouds blowing across the Missouri River floodplain from the east, and the wind began to pick up. The young robin heard several loud "chink, chink" calls and looked across the floodplain toward the river, where he saw a small flock of blackbirds rushing down the valley toward a warmer, more comfortable climate.

· · ·

Confused and indecisive, he moved hesitantly through the trees along the river, flying about twenty yards, stopping, then flying again, looking for berries, or other robins. Just after he landed on a dead cottonwood, he saw to his right, about a hundred yards from the river, a stand of cedar trees where a gently sloping rise between two lakes had formed when the river had changed its course in the past. A cabin at the base of the hill had a couple of cars parked beside it, and a path ran from the cabin to one lake. Another path ran toward the cedars.

The robin called out twice from his post on the cottonwood, but he heard no answer and saw no movement except for a couple of ducks cruising above the river. So he flew off, heading toward the cedars. He landed on one of them and saw pale blue berries hanging just above him. He fluttered up and grabbed one in his beak while hovering in the air, then hung on to the sagging branch and swallowed the berry. It was fleshy and somewhat dried but good. He struggled with a few more branches and finally gulped down about five of the berries in the steadily increasing wind. He was about to go after another when a slight movement in the cedar tree caught his eye.

He froze for a second, every muscle taut, poised for flight. Something was inside this thick tangle of tree limbs, but he couldn't make out anything or see any further movement. Curious, the young robin hopped up onto a higher branch and peered into the boughs. Scare! Two man-things were standing inside this square-shaped growth of trees. They were dressed in clothes with many oddly shaped patterns of tan, green, and black, and they were difficult to see. And each of them was holding something in his arms, a long, narrow object, round, hard, and small on one end and wider at the other. The narrower end was hollow and made of metal. The other end was made of wood. The men were smiling.

"George, if an old berry-pickin' robin can't see us from three feet away, there ain't a duck in the air that can spot us in this blind," said one of the men.

As soon as the man began to talk, the startled robin fled, not so much because he was afraid of men but because the unexpected presence of them so near frightened him. As the robin burst from the custom-grown and -shaped duck blind, tiny flakes of snow began to fall.

"Think I should take a shot at that robin, just to scare him?" asked one of the men.

"Okay, but don't hit him—we don't want to go around shooting robins."

The report from the shotgun did scare him, as did the rushing sound of the string of shot as it whizzed by him in the air, causing him to swerve to his right as he saw and heard the gray cloud zoom past about ten yards to his left. And just as he straightened out, he glimpsed two Mallards that had been flying toward the men in the duck blind. At the sound of the shot, the Mallards changed direction and climbed rapidly to get away from the confusing tangle of cedars below. The robin heard a human voice as one of the men swore at his bad judgment.

The Mallards passed to his right. Both species were moving out rapidly with the increasing wind blowing behind them.

All the robin wanted to do was to get away from that general area where he had been startled twice in the course of a half hour. With those experiences making him nervous, a storm now gathering force, and his migratory urge pushing him on, it wasn't long before he climbed above the treetops, aiming for the south but being blown more west than south by strong easterly winds.

The snow intensified as he flew. Beneath him he saw the tops of occasional trees, farm fields, and endless rolling grassland, sparsely populated except for herds of black-and-white and red-and-white beef cattle. Most of the trees were in valleys and gullies, on farmsteads, and along the occasional creeks and dry creek beds.

His instinct to move kept him in the air, but the wind had far more effect on where he was going today. It combined with the clouds and snow to make navigation impossible. Like a stick in rapids, he flew at its mercy west over Kansas into territory that became increasingly less well suited to robins.

By midday the young robin was fatigued, hungry, and thirsty. He had flown over several promising spots, but he had been afraid to put down because of the storm. Once it was because a lake, created by a large dam, was too wide, too expansive, and without enough trees on its shoreline for protection from the wind.

Another time he saw a wooded area along the banks of the Republican River, but just as he started to drop toward it a huge gust of wind nearly turned him over on his back. The gust blanked out the area below with snow and blew him past it in a couple of seconds.

He dropped lower to see the ground and trees more clearly. Just ahead he saw something that pleased him immensely. Not only did he see the river again, but he saw five robins heading in the same direction. He called out, but they did not return his call. He called again because he did not consider that they couldn't hear him because of the noise of their wing beats and the howling wind of the storm.

He was too fatigued to be able to put on a burst of speed to catch them, so he closed his wings and dropped, slowing his speed every few yards by opening his wings and tail. He landed on a shrub-filled, sandy island in the middle of the river. The storm was raging, but the young robin needed water urgently. He hopped and flew through the thick willow scrub that was trying to grow on the island, stopped briefly, and ran out onto the sand along the shore.

He drank deeply and looked about. On the far side of the river he saw an area of huge trees and thick undergrowth that began thirty to forty feet from the bank of the river and extended up a steep hill about fifty feet high. The woods appeared to stretch all the way up and down the river, but in the heavy snow it was difficult for him to tell. Quickly, he flew from the sandbar, crossed the river, and rose to the top of the hill. He landed on a telephone line and found himself amid a cluster of large stone buildings. Though it wasn't good hunting territory, the buildings did have a few spruce trees around them and they could provide shelter from the wind and snow.

Alongside one of the buildings the robin recognized pieces of bread, actually part of a sweet roll that had been dropped accidentally. The snow swirled around the bread, but the hungry robin flew to it and managed to rip off and swallow several large pieces before a man came too close, frightening the young bird away. He flew through the snow to a protected spot on a spruce tree behind the buildings, where he promptly fluffed his feathers up and dozed off.

Somehow he had the feeling that his hunting would be better tomorrow in this place. So he loafed away the remaining two hours until dusk and then slept soundly through the night. He awoke to find snow already melting from large patches of the roads, sidewalks, and lawns around him, and the ground was open and inviting, quite different from that snowy morning in Minnesota. It was still cloudy, and the clouds were low and moist, but they blew from the south and carried the promise of a warm and comfortable day.

He flew from the spruce to a utility line that stood higher than the building that had protected him but obstructed his view. From this perch, the young robin looked down along the river and to the other direction across buildings to a grassy field. Beyond it was a row of similarly sized and shaped houses with several spruce trees and many other trees and shrubs of various shapes and sizes. There was activity in the field, too. Walking around in the middle of it were a couple of starlings. He flew from the power line, over a building, and dropped down to a wooden post that stood alongside the field. To the post was mounted a sign that read: HEADQUARTERS AND HEADQUARTERS CO., UNITED STATES ARMY GARRISON, FORT RILEY, KANSAS.

The robin glided from the post to a damp spot near the field. After a few minutes he had partially satisfied his hunger by eating some light brown, kind of crunchy bugs that were alive but barely moving in the grass. From the grassy area, a parade field that was seldom used, he flew down a hill toward several cedar trees that grew along one side of another hill. There he found many light blue berries hanging from nearly every branch.

After eating his fill, he flew back to the power line near where he had spent the night. As he landed, he called, and off to his right he saw two adult robins heading toward the river. They answered him, and immediately he pushed off from the line, flying hard to catch up, following them over a couple of buildings and then down the hill in a steep descent toward the river.

Both birds were second-year adult males. They let him join them as they bathed in the river and then preened in the branches of one of the dozens of cottonwoods, the dominant tree in the woods. The three birds loafed and preened for nearly an hour. Then, with the two adults leading, they flew back up the hill to a thicket behind a cemetery near the other end of the parade field. The thicket consisted of thick, thorny shrubs called buffalo berries, hawthorns, vines, and an impossible tangle of weeds. There were dried berries everywhere, and it took the birds only a few minutes to eat their fill and hurry back to the river for more loafing.

The young robin had some difficulty keeping up with these two larger, stronger adult males in their prime. But even though he was fatigued from his migration, he managed to keep them in sight, catching up to them when they landed. He stayed with them for the rest of the day as they made more trips to the thicket to feed and then flew into a swampy collection of willows and cattails to spend the night.

It was then, as he closed his eyes while clinging to a gently swaying willow branch, low among the cattails, that he sensed his autumn journey was completed. This was where he would spend the winter.

He didn't know and didn't care that his sister was about 125 miles to the east, wintering in the farmland near Kansas City, or that his brother had flown two weeks earlier with a large flock of robins to a wet and wooded area near Calhoun City, Mississippi. Neither did he know that two of the robins he had traveled with during the summer were still on the shore of Lake Superior, eating mountain ash berries and bathing daily in the forty-degree water of the lake.

All he knew about, all he cared about, was that here, now, was the place where he lived.

WINTER

NOVEMBER BLENDED INTO December with little variation in the robin's routine. Daily the group, which had been joined by a five-year-old male and two yearling females, fed in the cedar trees that grew in the hilly land where the soldiers and tank crews trained. On warm days they often hunted in numerous grassy areas, seeking insects, larvae, and pupae. Food was available, but they had to put in their time to find it.

At night the birds would fly to the river to roost in the thick stands of willow saplings that emerged from dense, grassy undergrowth. When it was stormy, however, the young robin left the group and sought out the shelter of one of the spruce trees that had been planted widely throughout the fort. He felt more secure there.

From time to time one or two of the birds would stray from the group, and others would wander in from somewhere else to join them. But for the most part their number stayed between five and seven.

What a contrast in lifestyles! While the young robin's summer and fall had been pleasant and only occasionally difficult, winter was drab and hard. There were few new adventures or exciting chases. Instead, it was simply a tough period that required persistent effort to survive. The daily routine quickly settled into alternate periods of hunting, bathing, resting, and then hunting again, waiting out the dreariness of the days, trying not to expend too much energy, just existing.

Many people in northern parts of the robin range have visions of "their birds" basking through winter in a land of sun and warmth, a chamber of commerce version of Florida where the sun always shines, rich fruit falls from the trees, and the water flows cool, pure, and clean from the earth. On the contrary, for many robins winter means a harsh, cold, and sometimes cruel existence that brings death to the weak and unlucky and weakness to the strong. The enemies are adverse weather and a dwindling food supply that is never replenished during the dormant season.

As the winter wore on, the young robin and his companions put more pressure on the area's food resources, spending more time each day in pursuit of food. Their daily flights into the hills in search of berries became longer and less productive. And they often changed roosting spots, staying in dense cedar and vine tangles in gullies and ravines, conserving energy by avoiding the long flights to the river. But because the snow and rain that did fall usually dried up in a day or two, they still had to make frequent treks to the river for water.

When it stormed or just rained, which happened about every ten days or so, the birds remained still and passive in the shelter of the cedars, fluffed up to conserve energy and body heat. Occasionally, when it snowed, they took short flights to areas where dirt or grass might be exposed because of the wind. Mostly, though, they sat patiently and waited, facing the winds, moving a little, but riding it out to the end.

Thus December became January and the days became even colder and harsher. In the middle of the month, the five-year-old male disappeared. He simply was no longer a part of the group when it sought food in the morning, and the birds thought nothing of it.

What had happened was that the bird, weakened by his age (he was getting old for a robin, though they can live to be more than ten) and the diminishing food supply, had developed a lung infection that drained his strength. During the night the temperature dipped to zero, and this final insult was more than the weakened bird could handle. He tried to fluff up his feathers to fight the cold, but finally he fell to the ground, wheezing, and died as he tried to hide in the long, cold grass.

The young robin himself got a slight infection that caused him to wheeze. Though it made him uncomfortable, it was not painful, and it had only a small effect on his strength and stamina. But he did spend a couple of days hanging out in and near a huge brush pile created by flash floods in a deep ravine. He sat for much of the day in the middle of the ten-foot-high mass of branches and logs, fluffed up and dozing. He flew out to feed only three times during the day and became temporarily separated from the rest of the flock. The worst part of it was that every few minutes he had to open his beak and breathe very hard to keep the mucus from choking him. The sound, if you could hear it, would make you think that the robin had a bad cold. It sounded sort of like a sneeze.

But his strength soon came back, and on the morning after his second night in the brush pile he awoke and burst out of it, flying high with the wind in search of others of his kind. Within a few minutes he found them, feeding near a ravine about a quarter mile from where he had been recuperating.

For the rest of the week the birds remained in that general area, four miles from the river, feeding on berries and the occasional soft weed seed. The flock was lucky because though the weather was cold, with daytime highs only in the twenties, little snow or rain fell to chill them and cover up their food supply.

Once, in the first week of February, a fierce blizzard swept across the Kansas plains from Colorado, but the robins sensed it coming and flew back to the shelter of the woods and brush behind the Fort Riley stockade, where they found protection from the wind and blowing snow. They also found enough food to survive. It was spilled near the garbage cans behind the stockade dining areas and also in the post exchange parking lot. Oh, it wasn't the most nutritious food, but the bread, doughnut crumbs, and French fries dropped here and there kept the birds warm, full, and energetic. Without this food, one or two of them would probably have died.

It was after this snowy spell had passed and the sun again emerged that the young robin felt a certain restlessness inside him. It seemed familiar but also strange, an urge to do something, but he didn't know what. The lengthening days were calling to him. Something was very different.

15

SPRING

ROBINS AREN'T INTROSPECTIVE, so the young robin wasn't puzzled by this strange new feeling that began to dominate his awareness as the days grew longer. He only knew that he was restless and felt nervous. He also was more aware of the sun—the longer days were comforting, and in the afternoon, in a sunny spot on a hill, he liked the warmth and turned to absorb the heat on his breast and neck.

He also felt himself becoming more aware of the movement of the sun across the sky, and at times he felt an urge to fly in the direction that the sun's daily progression indicated as it inched farther north.

The nights, too, were affecting him. On clear nights in early February the arrangement of the stars seemed more familiar, while at the same time their new positions seemed in tune with this entirely new and as yet undefined urge.

He had changed externally as well. By mid-February he was indeed a different-looking bird than the drab fellow that had flown to Kansas the previous fall. The dull tips of many of the feathers on his body had worn back, resulting in a breast that, when the sun shone on it, was a brilliant orange-red, the most distinguishing mark of maleness in robins. At the same time, the brown and grizzled feathers on his head and back had also worn, and they were now a deep, dark, grayish-black color.

He carried himself differently, too. His head was higher, and his breast stuck out a little more at times, as if he desired to make himself appear bigger than he really was. Of course, he really was a bit bigger than when he had flown down to Kansas. In spite of the hardships of winter, the young robin had found enough food to add more bulk to his body. He had actually increased in size and weight, growing from nine to ten inches and adding a half an ounce, mostly in breast and neck muscle.

Some of the younger robins, born later in the summer and without as much time to grow as he'd had, would actually need to put on more weight over the winter months than he did. But it was more difficult for them to accomplish that because they were lighter and not quite as vigorous as robins that were lucky enough to have been successfully raised in the first nesting. However, the odds were equalized to some extent since the first nest efforts of robins are generally less successful because of the great vulnerability of the nests to predators and storms.

The young robin was also changing in ways besides his appearance. He was getting an attitude. By day the small flock often became separated, with the males breaking off from the females and chasing, fighting, and swooping among themselves in mock and real (but brief) battles that had little purpose since nothing was at stake. But they weren't like the playful chases of autumn. There was a new intensity in each little disagreement, and each bird was trying to test his ability to be dominant over the others, completely messing up the well-accepted pecking order that had prevailed earlier in the winter.

The females, however, still seemed to be in their winter behavior, following the same patterns of feeding, resting, and quietly seeking shelter near the river at night. Finally, the males separated completely from the females.

Gradually the band of males grew larger, and by the last week in February there were more than a dozen on most days. Instead of sleeping by the river, the flock stayed in the ravines, often wandering quite far during the day, making flights of five or six miles or more. As the days became warmer and longer, the band sought the south-facing sides of hills, where insects were brought out of hibernation by the sun's warmth. However, fruit, when they could find it, was still important to their diet.

Twice their wanderings brought them to small towns where they found apples, brown and mushy from the alternate thaws and freezes. Each time the robins gorged themselves on the cold, damp fruit.

The wandering flock flew in a loose bunch. There was no set flight order for them, but the young male was often flying in or near the front. He enjoyed these wanderings. His new urges seemed somehow satisfied by being up high and making these sprints from place to place. The speed satisfied him, as did the steady rushing of air made by the wings of the flock and the sound as it passed his ears.

One day the flock had just flown over the roof of a two-story house when they saw an apple tree below and to the left. Three of the robins called simultaneously, and they all wheeled sharply, fanning their tails and folding their wings to lose altitude rapidly. Because of the acceleration of falling, it was an exhilarating maneuver and they called to each other as they dropped. After plummeting fifty feet or so, half of the birds began the process of braking their speed with brisk fanning strokes of their wings and tails. They landed in a hackberry tree that grew at the edge of this backyard. The others dropped immediately onto the apple tree and began to tear into the apples. One by one the rest of the flock joined them, and they spent the next two hours there, alternately feeding and resting.

Inside the home a retired feed mill worker saw the spectacle and said to his wife, "Spring must be here, honey. The robins are back." He didn't know that the birds had spent the winter only five miles away.

"I always see robins about March first," he told her.

And he did, but it was because that was the time when they wandered a lot and were aggressive and conspicuous. So it was a sign of spring, but in a different way than the man thought. And the date was March 2. In only three weeks the sun would reach the spring equinox and the days would finally be longer than the nights.

After filling themselves with apple pulp, the flock departed as if on a signal, wheeling and climbing to the west, heading back to a sheltered ravine on the prairie. After about twenty minutes in the air, the birds saw a draw with dense cedars and shrubs and settled in for the evening. But the young robin had a difficult time sleeping. He felt the warmth from the sweet south wind. It combined with the urges inside him, giving him a great restlessness and a need to go somewhere. He felt the urge to fly into the night, but he dozed off and on, sleeping fitfully, eager to go but waiting for yet another cue.

• • •

Suddenly, about two hours before dawn, he awakened with a start. One of the birds in the flock, a male one year older than he, had made the flight call. The rest of the male robins, scattered about the ravine, heard and understood what it meant. It was time to go. The wind was still blowing gently from the south and after a bit of calling and some scolding, all the robins flew out of the thicket, climbing into the night to the north, away from the moon, responding to a signal as ancient as time and as wondrous as anything in nature. Another migration was under way.

It was a reward in itself. The act of taking off from the ravine with the flock into the dark unknown was not frightening for the young robin. On the contrary, it seemed to be the only thing that could ease his edginess. This felt right, and the new drive that the migration gave him, the new experience of heading north into the night, away from the moon, actually gave him energy.

As the flock climbed, he found it easy to maintain his place with the other birds. One aid to staying with the flock was wing noise. A couple of times he drifted off to one side, but he could easily detect that he was getting away from the other robins because the sound and feel of their wing beats became less intense. Robins fly with deep, powerful strokes, but the beats of their wings are not constant—that is, there is a delay in their wing beats, which permits them to hear the sounds of the other birds in the flock while migrating and thus helps them maintain their place with the other birds. Another auditory signal is the occasional call the robins make at times during flight—a loud, reedy call that is usually made and then immediately repeated. Several times during the first hour the young robin felt it within himself to call to the members of the flock. It was as if he was saying, "I'm here. I'm part of this." And when he did call, one or two others might answer, keeping the birds together with their instinctive behavior.

Sight was important, too. The young robin could easily make out the forms of the others in his group, though it was hard to distinguish their identities. His eye was attracted to many things: the white tips of the tail feathers of the others, the glowing, white-blue lights of farmhouses below, yard lights that made trees, buildings, and the occasional dog and early-rising man going out to milk the cows visible in the predawn darkness. As soon as they were fifty feet high he could see to the west and behind him the lights of Fort Riley. The main post area was a maze of bright beacons, and the outlying posts were lit up too, though not so much. In just a couple of minutes he was higher yet, and the lights of the town of Manhattan came into view, its airport beacon rotating white and green, and below on the road he could see the moving pair of eyes of a truck, bouncing, vibrating, and whizzing along on its own kind of journey. Back to his left, curling away from him, he recognized the familiar twists and turns of the Republican River, glinting and shining in the moonlight. Ahead he could see the dark shapes of the gently rising and falling hills, the rolling central prairie that was itself a landmark.

The moon lit the land dimly but plainly. With the stars shining brightly and the soft, warm wind blowing from behind, it was a perfect night for migrating. The robins responded to it by rising higher and higher until they leveled off nearly 250 feet above the Kansas prairie. On they flew, calling, working, twisting and turning, heading home. They knew they were heading someplace, but at this point in the migration, in the robin mind they knew only that they had a journey to make, and completing it was all that mattered.

• • •

After an hour of cruising north-northeast, the robins saw the gradual lightening of the eastern sky and responded to it by turning east for a few minutes to greet the sun before heading north again as the pink hue of the dawn reflected off their wings. Gradually the color spread over the sky and across the earth, with the hills and treetops lightening first and then the plains and valleys. Finally the sun broke the horizon, and shadows, like magic, sprang from the trees and buildings below. The robins kept the rising sun immediately to the right of their wings for the next hour and twenty minutes, and then, growing tired, hungry, and thirsty, they began to descend. Slowly at first and then quite abruptly, the birds dropped to treetop level, paused for a few seconds in a stand of scrub oaks, and then scattered out on a south-facing hill to search for insects.

The young robin was tired from the three-and-a-half-hour flight. He had burned up some of the small amount of fat he had accumulated during the later days of winter. The muscles of his breast and sides stiffened a bit, and he wanted to rest and preen. But food had to come first.

For several minutes he hunted along the hill. The only insects he could find were two small spiders that had just emerged from beneath a rock in response to the warming sun and the warmer air blowing in. Once he heard the danger call uttered softly by another of the robins about twenty feet down the hill, and at the same time he saw movement above as a big Red-tailed Hawk circled toward the north in a series of clockwise loops. But the hawk posed little threat to the young bird and his companions. The robins were instinctively confident of their ability to out-fly this large predator. Besides, the hawk was at a safe distance and at a range that would not surprise the robins.

Near the robins on the hill were a couple of other early migrants, a pair of strutting male Western Meadowlarks. The larks, busy eating seeds that had fallen from the native grasses the previous autumn, were unconcerned with the red-breasted intruders that had joined them on the trek north.

The land was free of snow, but insect life was far from abundant, and the birds had to expend a great deal of energy hunting to find only the scantest bits and pieces. The young robin hunted across the side of the hill, enjoying the warmth of the sun but feeling uncomfortable because of the stiffness in his breast and wings and the emptiness of his stomach. At the beginning of a steep slope where the hill started to drop away he spied a hawthorn thicket near a washed-out gully. One bush was loaded with wrinkled, dried fruits, and the young robin cried out with delight as he pushed off into the air and made five quick beats before beginning the downhill glide that would carry him to his meal.

A hawk! It was close. As he looked back toward the hill and most of the flock he saw a Red-tailed Hawk speeding low from the north toward the feeding robins. It was the same hawk they had seen before. It had apparently flown off to the north, dropped down, and was now making a low-level attack, using the peak of the hill to hide its approach. The young robin cried a warning and darted into the middle of the hawthorn bush, where he knew he would be safe. The robins back on the hill, hearing his warning call, were alert but could not see the onrushing predator. Instantly, as the hawk broke over the top of the hill, the startled robins and one of the two meadowlarks scattered. The hawk veered to its left and thrust its talons at a three-year-old male that, in a moment of indecision, had started toward the left and then stopped to turn in the other direction where there was more cover. Just as the robin changed direction, the hawk struck it. A puff of feathers flew from the robin, and the hawk skidded to a stop in the short, dry grass, dragging both wings and tail along the ground. It sat for a minute, looking over the sky and earth, then cocked its head to look at its prey. It blinked, then rapidly began tearing the breast feathers from the robin, exposing the skin and the dark red breast muscle beneath.

While it is true that the rodent-eating soaring hawks like Red-tails don't often feed on birds, their usual prey is not always available. This is especially so in late winter and early spring after winter has taken its toll on all life. The hawk takes whatever it can get, and populations in abundance bear the brunt of its predation. So it was that an older robin, tired after a hard winter and a sustained three-and-a-half-hour flight, became sustenance for a migrating female Red-tailed Hawk.

Just as the hawk swallowed the first piece of meat from the breast it was startled by a whirring noise about three feet to its left. The other meadowlark, which had crouched spread out, frozen in place, finally panicked and flew. Though the hawk was surprised by the noise, it was not interested in further pursuit. It had its prey and would consume it before hunting again.

The robins knew that too, or at least they were satisfied that the threat of immediate attack was over. Hurriedly, the scattered birds flew in a circuitous route about forty yards from the feeding hawk. The young robin, still sitting and quietly scolding in the midst of the hawthorn, saw three of the robins fly overhead. He called out to them, then pushed off from the hawthorn, leaving the massive feast of berries behind. He was nervous from the hawk's attack and uncomfortable with the general area.

In a few minutes he and the three others had joined six more birds from the flock, and after a fifteen-minute flight, about seven miles, they found another ideal south-facing hill. Just over the top of the hill stood several good-sized cedar trees, most of them with withered fruits still dangling from the branches. It looked like a good place to spend the day.

PART 3

ADULTHOOD

SPRING

T HE ROBINS STAYED in the area for three days. The time helped the young robin overcome the stiffness that the first flight had caused, and he could now fly without discomfort. It was a good place to stay. The living was easy for the birds, with ample bitter but nourishing berries and plenty of opportunity to find the insect life that was responding to the warming days of spring. Then, a weak cold front brought northerly breezes and clear, cold nights, and on the second night the temperature dropped to fifteen degrees. But the sun's rays were striking the earth with such energy that the daytime temperature of the ground on the hill rose to sixty-five degrees, even though the temperature of the air just above it was only fifty degrees.

Even earthworms were moving to the upper layers of the soil in spots. It had been a long time since the young male robin had eaten an earthworm. How it pleased him to pull one out of the ground, shake it, and gobble it down. How filling and pleasurable it was to have such a massive bulk of food slide down his throat into his stomach. But how quickly the worms were digested.

Despite the comforts of this spot, though, his restlessness returned, as did his feelings of aggressiveness. Several times as the flock was feeding on the hill he found himself fighting with another male for no apparent reason except a feeling that the bird was too close to him. Often when another robin wandered near him he was able to chase the bird away without a skirmish.

On the other hand, he found himself on the receiving end of similar attacks. To avoid a fight, the young robin usually turned and either ran or flew away, aware that he had strayed too close to another.

In spite of these sporadic hostilities, the band of robins stayed together in the same vicinity until, finally, they all left together. It was not the same kind of departure that they had made in their first flight. This time it began on the morning of the fourth day, after the birds had awakened and fed briefly on cedar berries. The young male had been the first one to finish feeding, and he was sitting on the ground near a puddle at the bottom of the hill. He had completed his bathing and drinking activities and had waded again into the puddle to take another bath, even though he had just preened himself and oiled all his feathers. Suddenly the other robins in the flock began to mill about, flying back and forth among the top branches of the thicket. He felt an overwhelming urge to join them and flew up from the puddle, climbing to the north toward them. Just as he got there, an older robin cried out and all the birds took off toward the north.

He was set to land at the instant they took off, and because of the attitude of his body—wings and tail fanned and vertical to the horizon, feet extended and aimed right at a branch—he was forced to land and immediately take off again. The main part of the group was about twenty yards ahead of him. The robins called to each other as they resumed the forceful but energy-saving strokes that identify robins (and most other thrushes) in flight. He flew hard to catch up to the others and then fell in place at the rear and on the right-hand side of the flock. They were not flying high; none of the birds seemed to want to today. The wind was blowing lightly from the southwest and the sky was clear. For some reason, an altitude between fifty and a hundred feet seemed right for the northward-moving flock.

After they had flown a couple of miles they saw two other robins high above them, heading east. The young robin saw them first and called out. Immediately one of the higher birds called back and closed his wings to drop a hundred feet or so to join the northward-moving flock. The other robin kept flying toward the morning sun.

Later the birds could see that they were going to be intercepted by a large flock of small birds moving toward the northwest. It was a mix of Snow Buntings and longspurs, late migrants for their species. Of course, the young robin didn't know what they were, but he saw that they were smaller and darker and showed flashes of their white feathers, and he could tell they were not a threat. The Snow Bunting–longspur flock numbered nearly a hundred birds, and in seconds they danced through the little band of robins, their undulating flight, rapidly whirring wings, and whistling flock call confusing the larger birds. Almost as if on a signal, the band of robins closed their wings and dropped nearly twenty feet to avoid the

Arctic-bound migrants. The young robin did a quick zigzag, veering left, right, and left again with half-closed wings, then plummeting with his wings closed and steering with his tail to get away from the intruders. In a matter of seconds clear air separated the flocks, and the robins watched the Snow Buntings dance and hop off into the distance. Bouncing, twisting, and turning, the buntings pursued their course, the flock becoming an organism in itself. Into the distance it went, finally appearing to be a bouncing gray-and-white mass that twinkled in and out of the range of his vision, then disappeared completely.

There were other encounters as well. Several times the robins passed near Kestrels cruising north, but the small, colorful falcons did not appear to be interested in pursuing the large, fast robins.

Once the flock was overtaken by eight Mallards, four drakes and four hens that flew between the robins and the sun, casting a brief shadow. But the Mallards, flying at nearly twice the speed of the robins, quickly passed out of sight.

To his right the young robin saw another flock of birds, undulating somewhat like the Snow Buntings but with greater ups and downs in each bird's flight. It was a group of Red-winged Blackbirds, all males, a familiar species to him and one that posed no threat. They were racing each other north to get the best possible nesting spots. This group was headed for the many prairie sloughs near Watertown, South Dakota.

After an hour in the air the young robin noticed a familiar uncomfortable feeling inside, one that told him the weather was changing. Ahead the birds could see a dark, overcast sky, a signal that they should stop and feed. Almost in unison, the band changed course slightly and dropped toward a stand of trees that stood out in this region of gently rolling hills and open spaces. From a distance of a mile the robins could see houses with evergreens, shrubbery, and trees that promised food and shelter, a robin refuge constructed by the intruder on the prairie, man.

The flock landed in box elder trees on the edge of a town that was near the Kansas side of the Kansas-Nebraska border. They immediately spread out on the lawn below, each bird hunting and hungry. The young robin glided to a grassy area behind one of the older white frame homes, built in the early 1950s. Two other robins sat in the trees at the edge of the yard as if undecided about what to do. The young robin landed on the grass, which was just beginning to turn green, and began his runs.

One of the other robins pushed himself off his branch and glided to black clumps of dirt in a garden in the neighboring yard. His companion in the tree sat for another few seconds watching the apparent lack of success of his two flock mates. Then he called out and flew to the base of a twelve-foot-tall Scotch pine growing near the door of a house about halfway down the block.

The young robin followed him, knowing that the lawn where he'd been hunting was barren. He landed near the other bird and immediately began eating—bread crumbs. It had been a long time since he had seen any, but he remembered that they were satisfying. He swallowed three crumbs and was about to eat another when the sound of air rushing through small wings interrupted him. He and his companion were joined by four male and three female House Sparrows. Brash and bold, the sparrows moved in on the larger robins and began to quarrel over several chunks of bread. The young robin, upset by the activity, turned away from the hullabaloo and went to pick up a piece of bread several feet from the sparrows. He shook off a couple of bites and was about to reach for another when, to his utter and complete amazement, one of the female sparrows hopped underneath his head, snatched up the bread in her beak, and flew out from beneath the pine toward a severely trimmed honeysuckle bush growing near the garage of a neighboring backyard. This was the first time in the robin's life that the pecking order of the largest first had been violated. He was so taken aback that he didn't make a move to chase the thief. Instead, he just stood there, as if dumbfounded, and watched her fly away.

After a few seconds he moved to one side, picked up another piece of bread, and flew toward the middle of the yard. When he got into the open, he glided slowly and landed on the grass, far from the pine, the bushes, and the House Sparrows. Then he shook off a morsel, swallowed it, and glanced around to see if another sparrow was going to try to steal the rest of his prize. A male sparrow did land nearby, but the robin quickly picked up his bread and ran away, stopping only when he was fully five yards from the would-be thief. The sparrow, realizing that he didn't have the element of surprise working for him, flew back under the pine to look for other crumbs.

As the young robin ripped the pieces from the crust and swallowed them, he noticed the sky darkening and saw thick, wet clouds lumbering in from the southwest, low and threatening. Thirsty, he flew to the top of a garage and saw a puddle in the street in front of the house. He flew to the puddle, drank, and bathed, then flew back to the pine, landing in one of the branches near the middle of the tree, about six feet from the top. There he preened, uncomfortable all the while because of the strange feeling inside him. And just as he dried off, rain began to fall, scarcely touching him through the thick branches of his cover. With the rain came a strange purring sound as thousands of tiny balls of sleet began to pour from the sky.

Some of the sleet got through the protective branches of the pine and stung the robin, so he hopped on down through the branches and joined his traveling companion on the ground. The branches gave them shelter, and there they remained for the rest of the day as the sleet turned into freezing rain, coating everything and taking a deadly toll on wildlife.

Sixty-five miles to the north, the eight Mallards, their urge to migrate stronger than their other senses, attempted to reach the Platte River during the ice storm, but the ice built up on their wings and backs, forcing the birds to the ground. One of them broke a wing as it crashed in a grazed pasture. But all of the ducks managed to walk to a protected weed patch in a low spot, and there they slept through the day, waking and shaking often to keep the ice from building up on their wings. The next day seven of the Mallards would take off again, leaving their flightless companion behind to an uncertain fate. He tried to go with them, but the pain in his wing was severe and he could not use it.

The two robins watched the freezing rain gradually turn to very light snow. They hopped up the branches of the pine tree and snuggled close to the trunk to sleep. They were still warm inside, thanks to the bread that had been put out for them.

17

SPRING

A LOUD CRASH RIPPED through the silence of the night, waking the young robin with a start. A limb of a brittle box elder tree, so common in prairie towns, had been overloaded with ice and had peeled away from the trunk. It was still dark, an hour or so before first light, but the reflected light from the snow gave the birds a view of the world that would be causing them trouble soon.

Everything was covered with ice, then snow, including the deeply sagging branches of their pine tree, which drooped more like a weeping willow than a sturdy pine. The power lines that ran down the street, clearly visible in the brightness that radiated from a corner light, now hung several feet lower than they had the night before. And they glittered from their icy coating as they swayed gently with the slight breeze that now blew from the north.

Everywhere the young robin and his companion heard a soft tinkling and swishing as ice beads fell on roofs and branches and into the snow below, breaking loose because of the flexing of the wood and power lines in response to the breeze. It was a musical but threatening sound. Strangely, the young robin began to sing. To his surprise, three notes of his spring song came from deep within him. Then he gave a soft warning call, tucked his beak beneath his wing, and went back to sleep, joining his companion in the security of sleep beneath the protective canopy of the pine branches.

Dawn came, and the stark reality of daylight made the world look even worse. Several inches of snow covered the ground. Beneath the snow on the trees and bushes, ice coated much of the landscape. The robins were safe and dry near the pine, but their hunger overcame their desire to sit and wait. They were very much in need of food to replenish the energy they'd expended in their migration flight the previous day.

If they had been back by Fort Riley they probably would have stayed in

----

or near the tree until later in the morning. But the hard winter plus their migration effort had drained their reserves. The young robin and all the other migrants like him, trapped by this storm, needed food now. Those who couldn't find it would grow weak. Those already weakened by the migration, the winter, age, or disease, probably would die if they couldn't find food sometime during the first or perhaps the second day.

The young robin looked around, then hopped down through the branches of the pine to the earth below. In spite of the protection from the tree, even here two inches of snow covered the ground, and the robin could not find any sign of the bread that he'd thought might be there. He took five slow steps, drawing one foot up into the warmth of his breast feathers at every opportunity, but he found no trace of bread or crumbs. Once he saw a lump that looked like it might be a crumb covered over by snow. Instead it turned out to be a dead sparrow that had suffocated because of ice plugging its nostrils as it struggled to survive the night near a gutter on the house.

Disappointed, hungry, and fluffed up because of the cold, the young robin just stood in the snow for two minutes. Then he flew out from beneath the tree, calling to his companion to join him. The two birds flew to the upper branches of a stunted box elder that grew across the alley from the yard where the pine tree stood. From their vantage point they rested and watched, looking for other robins feeding, looking for anything that might resemble fruit on trees or bushes.

The world beneath them was starting to stir. The robins saw lights flick on in houses, the bright change in the light intensity coming from the windows drawing their attention. They saw a young man emerge from one house and begin shoveling a path though the six-inch snowfall from the house to the street. The temperature had already risen above freezing and the snow and ice in the trees began to melt. But for the young man, the warming temperature made his difficult work even harder as he sweated under the exertion of moving the heavy, moisture-laden snow.

Before long he had cleared a path from the house to where his car was parked on the street, and he walked back into the house. The young robin was attracted to this clear place, thinking, somehow, that there might be food there. So he left his companion, flew down to the cleared sidewalk, and landed. He sat there for a few minutes. Looking. Listening. Waiting for some sign of insect life. He had learned that worms sometimes wash onto pavement after a rain. But his recollection tricked him today. There were no worms anywhere.

Suddenly the door of the house opened again, and the young robin flew into a tree across the street. The man came back out. He carried a suitcase in one hand and offered the other to help his wife down the steps. She was pregnant and they were on their way to the hospital. She saw the young robin.

"Look, Del, there's a robin, poor thing. When you get home throw them some bread. They probably can't find anything in this snow."

Her husband laughed. "Here you are, thirty miles away from the hospital, having contractions, facing icy roads, and me with no snow tires, and you're worried about the birds. I wonder if I can even get you to the hospital."

"Wait here," she said, and she turned and walked back into the house.

He tried to get her to come back, but she went into the kitchen, grabbed five slices of white bread, tore it into chunks, took a handful of raisins and some piecrust she had been saving, and threw it all on the sidewalk and steps.

"Now we've involved ourselves with more than one life today," she said as she came back to him.

He just laughed, shaking his head as he helped her down the sidewalk into the car. "That's one of the reasons why I love you," he thought, but he didn't say it—though perhaps he should have.

The young robin sat in the tree as the car spun off, weaving and slipping down the road. He felt uncomfortable and anxious to fly someplace, but he was still curious about the sidewalk and felt that it was the best place he could go to right now, especially since the humans had left. Just the fact that it didn't have snow on it was some consolation.

The young robin watched his companion fly down a couple of blocks to seek food in another neighborhood. But he himself was attracted back to the sidewalk, and as he landed he felt delight at the sight of the raisins and bread. He gobbled down bits of bread to ease his hunger. After that, he ran over to the raisins and picked one up in his beak. He had never touched or seen one before, but it looked very much like the fruit that he had been living on for the past several months and it tasted sweet and delicious. Quickly he swallowed it. It was good, and he downed four more of them, drank from a pool of water that had collected near the end of the sidewalk, and then ate a couple of bites of piecrust. He didn't eat more, even though it felt good, because his stomach was full.

For several minutes the young robin stood on the sidewalk, digesting his meal and drinking water from the slow melt of the snow. Then he flew up into the branches of an old soft maple, where he sat for several minutes more, looking, waiting, impatient because the ground was covered with snow and his eagerness to move north had been temporarily interrupted. His instincts told him that as long as snow was on the ground his survival would be difficult and it was better to expend energy in search of food than to burn it by migrating farther north, where in all likelihood he would encounter even more snow cover.

The young robin flew down to a clothesline a couple of houses away from the feast on the sidewalk. From there he flew to a patch of clear ground under the eaves of a large old house. The wide-spreading eaves had kept the snow accumulation there light, and already it had melted, leaving an open strip of ground about three and a half feet wide along the length of the house.

The robin ran a few steps, looking for insects in the grass, but he didn't find anything. It did seem to be warmer here, and drier too, so he simply stood and looked, occasionally running up and down the length of the earthen patch hunting for nonexistent insects. After an hour he flew back to the sidewalk where the food had been, but by now most of it was gone. Two other robins, plus some grackles, House Sparrows, and starlings, had moved in after he had fed and gobbled up most of the bread and piecrust.

But a few raisins remained. The robin ate four, drank more water, and returned to his dry piece of ground down the street. He spent the rest of the day flying between the warm ground and the sidewalk and finally swallowed the last raisin about an hour before dark. Then, knowing that the food supply was gone for good, he leaped off the sidewalk and, stretching his wings deep into the air, climbed almost straight up to the tall branches of the maple. Twice he called out. The second time he heard an answer from another robin flying about a block away. The young robin called to this distant bird and began to fly after him. But after flying about a hundred yards, he saw a good-sized spruce tree growing at the side of an old brick church. He landed on the top of the church and looked around for problems. It seemed safe, so he silently flew into the protective branches of the spruce. It was beginning to get cooler, and though the temperature was still above freezing, the young robin puffed up his feathers to keep out the cold. Then, just sitting there, he opened his bill slightly and sang a soft, quiet song for about ten seconds. It wasn't loud, but it was pleasant to him and made him feel good.

Then he tucked his beak under his wing and closed his eyes.

18

SPRING

FOUR DAYS HAD passed and the robin was still in the small town. Each day was warmer than the previous one, and the melting snow made drinking puddles available everywhere. On the third day, large areas of grass began to appear as the snow slowly melted away.

For the first couple of days the young robin was dependent on hand-outs, as were many other birds in the area. The people of the town had not planted many fruit-bearing trees or shrubs, especially the kind that held their fruit until the spring months. As a result, about 15 percent of the robins waylaid by the spring storm had perished. Because of the lack of food and low fat reserves, they were simply unable to generate enough body heat to stay alive. But they were in the vanguard of the migration, the early birds, the risk takers. Behind them, from Texas, Oklahoma, Louisiana, and elsewhere, would come thousands of robins to fill the voids left by these birds.

Other early-migrating songbirds fared better—the grackles, black-birds, meadowlarks, and native sparrows and juncos could get by eating the seeds of native weeds and grasses. Though a few perished, most were able to find sustenance during the hard days following the storm.

As the grassy areas emerged, the robin scurried about, joining others of his kind on the higher, warmer knolls, seeking and finding small insects warmed back to activity by the sun. By the fourth day after the storm the ground was a great deal drier, and the robins that had survived the storm were able to find enough of their natural food to stay alive.

Once again, as the threat to their survival diminished, the robins began to feel restless. The young robin was nearly overwhelmed by the urge to fly. He again became aggressive and belligerent in his anxiety, chasing and bickering with the other robins he had joined.

On the young robin's fifth day in the town he awoke an hour and a half before dawn. With several other robins, he had taken refuge for the evening in a dense tangle of bushes and trees growing on the north side of the town. The tangle was the overgrown remnant of a windbreak planted by a farmer in the late 1930s, after the great drought. The house that it had been protecting was long since gone, but the tangle remained, providing cover for several kinds of birds throughout the year, including a small covey of Bobwhite Quail.

Flight was all the young robin could think of. He looked at the sky, saw the stars shining everywhere, and then heard a couple of small scolding robin sounds as others in the flock awakened too, responding to the same urge.

To his own amazement he pushed off from the branch on which he had been sleeping, calling to the others to join him. In the thickness of the tangle, his left wing twice beat upon branches as he flew nearly straight up through the darkness. He heard other wings flapping and slapping branches too, and he knew that he was not alone on this journey.

In fact, the entire flock of robins, now numbering an even dozen birds, had awakened at nearly the same time, each eager to migrate. The call of the young robin was all the inspiration necessary for each to begin its response to this powerful drive, this special memory of birds that enables them to anticipate future food supply.

The flock climbed steeply out of the tangle, spread themselves over an area thirty yards wide, and began cruising to the north, climbing to put nearly four hundred feet of air between themselves and the ground. Even now, as they climbed into the blackness, their sensitive eyes could detect a very gradual lightening toward the east. In no time at all the sky began to turn pink, then reddish pink, then blue as the warm yellow sun edged over the horizon.

Calling to each other seemed to encourage their exuberance as the early-morning light surrounded them. Several times, for no reason other than the delight of it, the young robin wheeled, first left, then right, closing his wings and diving rapidly only to open them with a rush of air and zip back up to the altitude of the flock. Once while he was engaged in this maneuver, another of the robins chased him, and he wheeled nearly straight up in flight to position himself behind the other bird so that he became the chaser, diving at his tormenter in mock battle and snapping his bill with the excitement of the chase. But this was wasting energy.

The birds settled into more-normal flight and after a couple of hours began to feel some fatigue. Still, they pressed on toward the northeast. Ahead, the young robin saw a thick, winding band of trees on both sides of rapidly moving water. As the birds got closer they saw that the water looked brown, though some pools near the sides, fed by snowmelt, seemed more blue and appealing. The thirsty and hungry birds quickly descended toward one of these puddles. Most of them landed in the top of a large tree before dropping to the puddle to bathe and drink, but the young robin and another yearling plummeted immediately to the shore of the pond. The sound of the air rushing past their wings and tail as they braked for landing made a young thirteen-striped ground squirrel rush for cover, frightened at this sudden intrusion during his first foray for food since he had awakened from hibernation earlier that morning.

• • •

The young robins paid no attention to the rodent; they merely drank their fill from the shore of the pond. Off to one side of the backwater swam a pair of Pintails, quietly minding their own business as they poked around the submerged grasses looking for tender, succulent roots. In the mud flats on the far side, three Killdeer bobbed and ran back and forth looking for snails and insect larvae to give them energy for their migration.

The young robin drank deeply several times, then flew to a high branch on a cottonwood growing back from the river on higher ground. Several other robins went to drink as he began to preen and groom his feathers. He wasn't very stiff or sore and still felt a great urge to move on. But he was somewhat reluctant to do so on his own, so he sat and preened and watched the others drink and run in the mud on the shore of the pond. Restlessness soon began to overpower his other feelings, however, and he felt increasingly agitated. He showed his feelings by calling and scolding as he hopped around the branches on the tree, flitting his wings to a partly open position and flashing his tail in almost the same movement.

Finally, he could stand the tension no longer and he called out, pushing off from the tree and flying strongly up the river channel. He had to go on. The instinct to migrate had overpowered his need to be with others of his kind. However, as he called back he noticed another young male following fifty yards behind him.

Luck had been with the young robin during the storm, but his companions had not fared as well and thus they did not feel strong enough to continue the trek north. They had not stumbled upon stores of bread and raisins, and now they, except for the one young robin that followed, needed to build up reserves before continuing their migration. So they just watched as the two flew out on their own, turning as they cleared the last few shrubs growing on the river bottom, following the river north.

The two robins gradually climbed and, after following the river channel for about a mile, turned slowly to the right, leaving the river and its concentrations of birds and predators behind. Although the robins hadn't seen any enemies, predators were along the river bottoms in abundance. The bird-eating hawks and owls, in particular, were roosting and resting along the water simply because of the abundance of prey. Waterfowl, Red-winged Blackbirds, many sparrows and finches, and the early shorebirds were thick in the vicinity of this concentration of habitat and food resources. Because of their own migration, many hawks and owls stopped here to hunt. Birds unlucky enough to be weak because of poor nutrition during the later weeks of winter, or just unlucky enough to be unable to find ample stores of food during migration, became prey that was easier to catch, and helped nourish the Prairie Falcons, Sharp-shinned Hawks, and Cooper's Hawks that rested in the big cottonwoods.

Here and there along the river were other hawks, too, and a few Bald Eagles that had become adept at singling out the sickest ducks and dead fish—fish that died because of chemicals they'd ingested or because they got stuck in a shallow backwater and couldn't find a way out; ducks that were victims of diseases or still suffering from wounds they had sustained during the hunting season, not injured enough to die but too disabled or weak to effectively avoid a bird of prey.

But the two robins flew away from this concentration of creatures and turned northeast, away from the Missouri, toward the more wooded lands that lay far beyond the horizon. With the benefit of a moderately strong tailwind that increased with altitude, the robins gradually climbed until they were nearly a thousand feet high. At this height they were invisible to a man on the ground and higher than the hunting range of most of the hawks, which preferred to be lower to the ground and closer to more prey species.

Yet even at this altitude they were not alone. Their keen eyes detected a pair of migrating Swainson's Hawks soaring in increasing circles far to the east. And to the west there was a buzz of activity as various species of waterfowl poured back and forth along the open channel of the Missouri, some migrating flocks rising as high or higher than the robins were flying.

Silently the two pushed on as the sun moved across the mid-March sky. Their course carried them into southwestern Iowa. Beneath them they saw many hills and wooded areas with all but the most shaded spots free of snow. The few wetlands and stock ponds were free of ice, and the roads were busy as cars sped up and down the country lanes accompanied by the roar they made as they pushed the air out in front of them. It was so loud the robins could hear it above their wing noise.

Three hours passed and finally the birds began to tire and get the thirsty, hungry pain in their gut that demanded response. They had covered just over 100 miles since leaving the rest of the flock in the Missouri River bottoms, making their total more than 160 miles today alone. Though the robins measured their distances more by the feel of their muscles and the nearness of their goal, it was apparent to them that they had gone a long way. Each bird had lost weight, and now they needed food and water.

The young robins saw a creek, and both of them began to alternately close and open their wings, losing altitude rapidly but avoiding excessive airspeed. It took them only about a minute to descend and another ten seconds to find a spot on the creek bottom that looked like a good place to drink and rest.

There a spring that fed the creek bubbled up in a large, deep valley, sheltered on the west, east, and north by three large hills. A wide variety of robin-friendly micro-habitats grew in this bowl-like structure. At the point where the spring surfaced, the ground sloped gently. It was part of a pasture grazed by a small herd of black-and-white Holstein dairy cows. The farmer did not allow his cows to graze there continuously, and so the grass cover was moderately long and teeming with insect life. About a hundred yards beyond where the spring surfaced stood an old fence that marked the end of the pasture. There a thicket of willows grew for about thirty yards, running the length of the bowl. Beyond that stretched a hundred-acre patch of woods on steeply rolling hills. On one side of the pasture, where a hill sloped up to the north, stood three big old cedar trees, still holding dried-up, wrinkled (but appetizing to a robin) blue berries.

The area was one of many fine migration rest spots in southwestern Iowa and, while on the edge of the unplowed hill country that did much to provide wildlife habitat, it gave the robins everything they needed to restore their strength quickly. Water, insects and other bugs and worms, ample and readily available fruits as an emergency and supplementary food, and cover for safe, secure resting and preening.

It wasn't long before the two young robins had satiated their appetites, bathed, and flown to the cedar trees to preen and nap.

19

SPRING

NIGHT WAS UNEVENTFUL for the two robins huddled near the base of the protective cedars. But as the first light began to soften the eastern sky they awoke restless and nervous. Inside the young robin the urge to migrate was growing more intense as he put distance between himself and his wintering grounds and grew closer to his destination.

However, his first movements revealed some stiffness in his breast and wings, and a great hunger and thirst that needed attention.

Slowly the robin extended his left wing to its fullest, straining to stretch the small wing muscles and the larger breast muscles that controlled most of the motion of flight. Then he repeated the movement with his right wing, twisting, turning, and flexing the small muscles that opened and closed the primary feathers during flight. That seemed to help. Then he called once to his companion, hopped down a few branches, and flashed his tail a couple of times to work the kinks out of those muscles attached near the tip of his skeleton, just above the abdominal cavity.

He fluffed up his feathers and then, seeing some berries at the tips of the branches of the next tree, he flew across to them, fluttering and grasping to get some kind of a foothold on the wispy, floppy cedar.

He gulped down five berries, while his companion did the same on lower branches. Then the young robin flew from the cedars toward the spot in the meadow where the spring was bubbling out of the brown grass amid the moisture-loving plants that grew there. It took him only a few wing beats to accelerate to sufficient speed for flight, and then he glided down the sloping hill toward the pool into which the spring flowed. He landed on a large rock that protruded from the surface of the pool and tried to see its depth. He wanted to bathe but was reluctant to enter water that did not have a gradual transition from shallow to deep. The pool, largely because of its erosive effects on the soil during periods of high flow, dropped straight down at the shore and was fully eight inches deep, far too deep for any robin. He bent over, dipped his beak into the cold, dark liquid, and then raised it to the sky, delighting in the sensation of this icy water flowing down his throat. He took two more drinks, then leaped up from the rock, using his tail and wings to turn in midair, and followed the stream to look for a more suitable site for bathing. He flew about a hundred yards and had to enter the dense woods before he found what he was looking for. He closed his wings, dropped five feet, then landed on a three-foot-long bar of gravel that was exposed in the middle of the creek. It was perfect. It gradually sloped into the water, allowing the robin to pick the right depth for a bath. It didn't take him long. Immediately it looked as if he was having a water fight. It was almost impossible to see him because of the spray from his shaking head and his flapping, half-closed wings.

After he was thoroughly wet, he flew from the bar to a horizontal limb on one of the large oak trees growing in the patch of woods. There he preened and fluffed his feathers and scratched all the small places on his skin that itched, mostly because of the few lice that were living off his body oils. He felt good.

Then he sang, that wonderful robin song: Three notes. Pause. Two notes. Pause. Two notes. Three notes. Ending with a high trill. It was his first ever full-blown, all-out attempt at a song, and it surprised him in a way, though it made him feel good inside. As he was singing he remembered other songs, especially the one his father used to sing (though he couldn't recall his father), and he made an effort to make it sound kind of like that.

He was about to sing again when a flash of brown below caught his attention. Instinctively he froze, then slowly cocked his head to watch the long-bodied, short-legged creature hopping along in the shallow water of the creek, poking its head into every hole and looking under every tuft of grass that hung over the bank. It was a mink, the first the young robin had ever seen, but the robin sensed that this animal was a dangerous predator.

The mink bounded out to the sandbar where the young robin had landed and sniffed at the soil where the robin had defecated. The mink, a small female whose four young had been killed by a male mink (and not the one that had mated with her), raised her head in the air and looked into the trees to see if the bird she had smelled was still about.

At that moment the robin uttered his ground predator call, the soft, quiet, ominous string of tones that usually means cat. The mink stood on its back legs for a better look into the tree, and her dark eyes spotted the robin instantly because of the bird's habit of bobbing its tail when it gave the call. But the mink chose not to pursue. She knew that when it was obvious that a bird had seen her, an attack would be hopeless. If she started toward the tree she knew from experience that the robin would fly away. So she simply turned and continued down the creek, hoping for an early frog or crawfish, or an ambitious sucker that had survived the winter.

The robin, unafraid but concerned about this predator, gave his warning call and left. He called out, heard his companion answer, and then flew up through the oak's branches toward the open sky. After a couple of sharp turns to avoid the densest parts of the upper canopy, the robin climbed into clear air and turned again to the north, positioning the early-morning sun off his right wing. He called again and heard his companion answer from about a hundred feet behind. The birds slowly climbed but found the wind (which was blowing lightly from the east) more hindrance than help today, so they dropped to an altitude about twice the height of the mature trees.

A man or woman would have stayed in that little valley for a couple of days if he or she had the same wants and needs as a bird. Reason would have won the argument to rest and build up strength before continuing. But the robins were responding to a compulsion to return to a place like the one where they had learned to fly. It had to feel right, and look right, and have the same sky, and trees, and length of days and nights. Reason had nothing to do with how the robins were behaving. That's not to say that birds can't think. The robins had learned many things: Where to look for foods that nourished them. Where to sleep to avoid storms and predators. That high hawks were seldom a threat but low ones should be avoided. That some ground predators would try to climb trees. That berry bushes were often located in hilly terrain with water in close proximity (in the southern plains). And much, much more.

But when it came to their physical state, they couldn't move beyond what they could think and feel at any given moment. If a robin felt fine— no soreness, stiffness, illness, or wounds—then it was as fine as it could be. The power to reason beyond that, to consciously build up a reserve of fat and muscle strength for possible tough times ahead, was simply beyond their mental capability. Don't get it wrong. Birds can and do think ahead in time. They know that if they want to feed and then fly to a roosting area, they have to allow time to do both before dark. Or, when a bird leaves point A to go to point B, it has thought prior to leaving point A about point B and knows how long it will take to get to that destination. It's like saying, "Hey, I'm hungry! I think I'll run down to the hamburger stand." As you leave you subconsciously compute the time it will take you to get there and how to get there, and you also plan about how long the trip will take altogether so that you can make another objective decision, e.g., "Okay, but I've got to be back at seven. Company's coming." When birds are migrating, many of them know precisely where they want to go. Some birds don't get to their destination because they get lost; others may find a place that "feels" better. Others of the same species are wanderers or pioneers, following nature's plan to seek out and exploit all suitable habitats for the benefit of the species.

These two robins were headed to the northeast, to the mixed deciduous hardwoods where they were raised (even though those hardwoods were in a suburb). The young robin was being lured more and more by the emerging memory of the tall chimney that was such a prominent homing point during his early life on his own. As he and his companion flew along he began to look for it and the singular combination of trees and grounds around it that made it unique.

His companion, though raised in similar circumstances, was looking for something quite different. He grew up in the bottomlands where a creek had joined a large river. All his high-flying memories focused on that winding, shimmering waterway. That was what he looked for as the birds pressed north.

Instinctively both birds knew—they felt—that they had a long flight to go, but every mile they covered made them more excited about their destination.

Beneath them the hills gradually became broader and gentler. After a couple of hours they stopped for water at a small pond and then flew on, finally ending their flight after four and a half hours in the air to feed, bathe, and rest in the wooded hills along the Des Moines River.

The next morning, after watering at the edge of the river, the pair resumed their trek to the north-northeast. Again they flew for a couple of hours, stopped briefly in a flooded pasture to water in the cool ponds formed by the snowmelt, then continued on for a total of more than four hours' flying time. That amounted to more than 120 miles and brought the birds just beyond the Minnesota-Iowa boundary. The young robin sensed that he was very close to home, and he wanted to continue flying almost as much as he wanted to satisfy his hunger. But he and his companion were too hungry to go on, so they descended into a small farmyard, out by itself in the tilled black fields, an oasis to birds because of the thick shelterbelt planted years ago along two sides of the farmstead to break the powerful west and north winds.

It was a typical midwestern shelterbelt, two rows of shrubs on the outside (honeysuckles in this instance), a row of Russian olive trees, two rows of box elder trees, and then a row of spruce. A big white frame house stood nearest the shelterbelt, and downwind from it and to the east (because most of the winds blew from the west and northwest) stood the barn and other buildings once used for chickens and hogs. As was the case at many farms, the livestock were all gone except for a few bantam chickens kept largely as reminders of the good old days of diversified family farming. As the robins broke their flight and descended into the shelterbelt, they saw an old blue-and-white pickup truck head down the gravel drive and turn left onto the blacktop highway that ran north into town.

The young robin landed first, on a branch at the top of one of the box elder trees. He surveyed the scene below him, noting the mowed grassy area around the house, a flock of House Sparrows feeding on the ground near the new galvanized-metal machine shed, and an apple tree growing on the far side of the house. There were still a few apples hanging from it.

He dropped off the branch, falling nearly straight down for fifteen feet before tipping his tail and spreading his wings to direct himself toward the apple tree. His companion watched him from a branch in another box elder, then flew to the top of the house, landing on the brick chimney to watch the young robin feed.

The branch of the apple tree swayed up and down as the young robin inched his way out to its end, fluttering and hopping, trying not to lose his balance. Finally, after several near tumbles, he was next to an apple, though it hardly resembled the apple it had been. Instead of being red, with shiny skin and solid white meat, it was brown, with wrinkled skin and mushy meat. But to the young robin it was delicious.

He poked his sharp beak into the mush, getting a beakful of the meat, which he promptly swallowed. Then he did the same thing again and again, filling his stomach with the sour, delicious fruit.

Next he flew to the ground, wiped his beak several times on the grass to remove bits of pulp sticking to it, and began hunting for worms and insects. As he ran and paused in the brownish, dormant grass, his companion fluttered above him, working hard to get his nourishment from the apple tree.

The young robin did find a few small insects, mostly ants warmed by the midday sun, and one earthworm that had ventured to the top of the soil. After swallowing the worm, he flew to the roof of the house to look for water, spotted a puddle at the far edge of the driveway just beyond the end of the shelterbelt, and flew to it to drink and bathe. Bathing and drinking always felt good to him, but what felt even better was the rest he took afterward. He was tired from two days of sustained flight, and it wasn't long after preening that he began to doze on the limb of the box elder tree where he sat. The warm March sun felt good on his breast and head. It made him so comfortable, so warm, and so tired that he fell into a kind of trance, dozing, resting, waking, looking about, then dozing again, just a few seconds at a time.

For two hours he dozed, scanned for danger, then dozed again, finally waking up, somewhat stiff but rested and eager to move on. It was only about two thirty in the afternoon, but the farther north he got, the more intense was the pressure to keep moving.

He hopped down a couple of branches, flapping his wings to break his descent and to work out the stiffness. Then he called to his companion. His location call, two short notes, was answered by one note from the other side of the house. Quickly the young robin dropped out of the tree and flew at about five feet off the ground toward the house. He swerved to bank his turn around the side of the building, then saw his companion on the ground hunting. The young robin dropped closer to the ground by closing his wings, then spreading his wings and tail to brake his airspeed, landing at a run. He began to hunt about fifteen yards from his companion and in no time at all had pulled three worms from the earth. He also picked up a soft little bug that was attempting to hide beneath the grass. That seemed to satisfy his craving for protein. His companion, however, was still hunting.

The young robin leaped up from the lawn and flew in a steep climb to the peak of the house's roof. There he surveyed the area again, looking for anything that might be suspicious. This time the sparrows were gone. Movement overhead caused him to tilt and peer into the sky with one eye, but it was only a gray-and-white pigeon passing from a farm down the road to feed in a field beyond the farmstead. The robin glided to the apple tree and again fought the tippy branches to get several swallows of the mushy brown fruit into his gullet.

A few strong beats of his wings brought him to the power line that ran along the driveway from the highway to the farmhouse. The robin sat on the line for several minutes, digesting his food and watching the other robin hunting in the backyard, still picking up worms and insects.

The urge to move north was strong. Finally he felt he had to go. He leaped from the power line and began climbing immediately, calling to his companion on the ground to follow. But the other robin needed nourishment and wasn't ready to leave. He stayed behind.

Craning his neck briefly to look back, the young robin saw the other bird still on the ground, a tiny speck as he passed beyond the shelterbelt over the wet and somewhat muddy black fields below. He felt no remorse at leaving his temporary companion behind. He only knew that he had territory to claim, that it was to the north, and that he had the strength and power to fly there now.

He flew for two more hours, passing over scores of farmsteads like the one that had provided him shelter for a few hours. Here and there on the landscape below were pastures and woodlots, remnants of the days when so many farms had a few dairy cows. Some of the unnaturally straight lines of cover provided by drainage ditches had given way to stands of elm and cottonwood, the elms now bare and brittle, their life taken from them by Dutch elm disease. Most, though, were simply patches of grass and shrubs that provided false cover—they were so narrow that all the predators in the vicinity hunted them ruthlessly, virtually eliminating the ground- and shrub-nesting birds that tried to live in them.

Here and there he saw a patch of woods near wetlands or on a hillside that was too steep to plow. And as he got farther north, the size and frequency of these wooded hillsides increased. Twice he saw lone robins below him, sitting on trees at the edge of the wooded patches. And several times he saw hawks on the move, taking advantage of the afternoon currents and the fine day. He felt no threat and pressed on. Finally he flew over a large city that seemed lower to him; it was built on the floodplain of a vast river that was lower than the surrounding countryside. The wooded hills that climbed up from the city to the north looked like a good place to find food and water.

The young robin stopped to take water at a creek that was easily seen through the branches of the bare but heavily budded trees. After he drank he spent a half hour hunting diligently in a clearing at one side of the creek. It provided him with a few insects and one very weathered rose hip, the last one on a thorny bush at the edge of this field.

Although still hungry, he was tired, and he acquiesced to the approaching darkness and the night threats that this wild wooded area might bring. So he flew from the woodlands back to the south for a half mile, to the dense grasses and cattails that grew in the river floodplain. Silently the robin glided into the grassy slough as twilight stretched out its last orange fingers, streaking the gray clouds that whispered spring to all the living creatures in the area. He landed on a tall cottonwood sapling in the grass, then hopped down to the ground and into a dense buckthorn plant that was nearly impenetrable from any angle other than the one by which the robin approached it.

Thus shielded from the predators of the night, the young robin fell asleep. Before he dozed completely off, his last thoughts were about how familiar this area was, how much it seemed like a place he had known. The image of the smokestack flitted through his mind, and then he fell asleep.

SPRING

T HAT NIGHT THE young robin awakened several times. One reason for his unrest was the stiffness that lingered after the day's long flight, but most of his sleeplessness was because he was so eager to move on.

The fickle spring weather was deteriorating again, though, and the conditions were not good for migrating. He felt that inside as the barometer dropped, and when he looked up he could tell by the blackness that the sky was totally overcast, the worst situation for migration at night.

So he tucked his beak back under his wing, closed his eyes, and dozed away the hours until dawn. Finally it came, sooner than usual but with the early light hidden by dense clouds. As always, the young robin flew out to greet the light, bounding from his brushy tangle with a pair of loud calls and a flashing of his tail. Then he turned north toward a low-growing patch of cottonwoods that had sprouted in the floodplain. Once, in a dry year when the river was down, a farmer had plowed that field, thinking that perhaps he could sneak a crop of sweet corn from it before it got too wet to till. But his effort was a flop. The cottonwoods took advantage of the freshly opened ground, and nearly a thousand seeds sprouted. Now the surviving trees were all about twenty-five feet tall, so thick and fighting so hard with each other for light and nutrients that it seemed they would soon choke each other out and all would die.

At first the robin thought the thick stand of trees might offer berries or the damp ground beneath them would offer plenty of bugs or worms. But as he got close he saw the barrenness of this twiggy jungle and turned toward his right. Ahead lay the wooded hillsides that climbed up from the floodplain and, before the hills, a busy four-lane highway stretched across the land. The floodplain was, in fact, the bed of a great river formed at the conclusion of the last glacial period, ten thousand years ago.

The young robin saw nothing that appealed to him. Yet he was eager to eat something before moving on. He climbed a bit to see beyond the forested hills, didn't like what he saw (which was mostly plowed fields and farmsteads), and turned back toward the winding river. In two minutes he covered the mile that separated him and the river. He dropped down to its shore and flew along the sandy banks for about a hundred yards until he found a quiet, shallow pool that looked safe enough for drinking and bathing.

He drank a couple of swallows of the muddy water, rushed through his bath, then flew into the thick branches of a tall cottonwood about fifty yards from the river. As he preened and arranged his feathers, mist began to fall from the formless clouds. The fine droplets reduced visibility considerably and collected on every branch and twig, every boulder and blade of grass, changing the late March world into a damp and humid contrast to the sunny day before.

Overhead the robin saw a huge, dark hawklike bird with a white head flap its wings slowly, then turn toward the tree in which he sat. Frightened by the bird's menacing size, the robin sat frozen on his limb, prepared to flee but trusting that his stillness would keep his presence hidden from the bird of prey. What he didn't know was that the Bald Eagle had seen a dead carp floating down the river and was dropping toward it in steadily diminishing circles. The carp was to be the eagle's breakfast and would give it strength to continue migrating to the northern wilds of Minnesota.

As the carp drifted downstream, the eagle changed its course, slipping with the wind and away from the robin as it dropped closer to the water. And as the distance between them increased, the eagle became less of a threat to the robin. Finally, the robin bolted from the tree, flying again to the north, over the highway, toward the open land beyond. But this time he didn't go quite so far. There, on a hillside that appeared to have bubbled up out of the level floodplain, stood a stand of tall sumac bushes with a few dried-up fruits still scattered on them.

The hungry young robin closed his wings and plummeted toward the bushes, breaking his fall with outstretched wings and tail just before landing in the packed-down grass on the hill. Above him, about six feet high, stood the sumacs. He flew to one of the bushes, fluttering and clinging to the bending branch until he worked the fruit loose and got it firmly between his upper and lower beak. Then quickly he swallowed it, forcing it into his stomach with rippling contractions of his throat muscles.

Within a couple of minutes he had downed five more fruits. But though his hunger was cured, all the fluttering in the mist allowed some beads of water to work past his feathers, near the base of his wings.

The robin flew away from the sumac across a field and landed on a strand of a barbed-wire fence, where he sat and preened, working with his bill to break up the water beads, arranging and re-oiling his feathers. After a few minutes he was groomed to his satisfaction. He paused as if to get his bearings, then rose from the fence with a great leap and climbed to the north, leveling off at a low altitude that took him just above the trees, skimming through the topmost branches of some and avoiding the high branches of others. He was on his way home.

The young robin climbed the 150-foot hills that marked the perimeter of the floodplain. The mist didn't bother him much except for reducing his ability to see things at a distance. His eyes were so sensitive to gradations in light that he could detect the approximate location of the sun most of the time. Occasionally a band of exceptionally thick clouds would pass by, diffusing the sun's rays so much that even the robin would get disoriented. But in these brief periods he had picked out landmarks to the north that allowed him to navigate without losing his direction.

On he moved, more to the northeast now than earlier in his migration. He felt exposed as he passed so low over the open fields, and often deviated from his course by several degrees to fly over trees. He felt safer over trees when he was flying low, for he knew that they could provide him a chance for retreat if he was attacked in the air. And the misty sky made him feel even more at risk today. Over a field, especially a plowed field with no place to hide, he could only rely on his strong wings.

For a long while he kept the thick forest that grew along the edges of the river in his sight, not only for safety but because the river paralleled his course. After he'd been in the air for an hour, the forest gradually slipped away into the mist, to be replaced by pastures and other woodlands as he continued to fly northeast. The mist grew thicker with each mile, and occasionally he saw patches of snow on the north sides of hills and shaded valleys where the rays of the sun did not shine directly.

The robin felt increasingly tired as he pushed toward his goal. But paradoxically, the closer he got, the more he wanted to get there. Despite his weariness, getting there—to that place—was everything. And he felt that today he would. Still, the weariness persisted. Several times during his second hour in the air he paused for short rests of twenty to thirty seconds in the uppermost branches of trees. But he pressed on eagerly after each rest stop.

The mist did affect his navigation a little as he flew on into his third hour in the air. His instincts were battling within him because of it. He knew—he felt—that he was near home, and he wanted to fly high to look for landmarks. But when he found himself climbing high he got nervous and tense as his view of the ground faded in the mist, so he dropped back down, skimming the treetops and resting even more frequently, but still pressing on. Often, though, he paused for as much as a minute. Twice he flew down to the ground to drink from puddles formed by the collecting moisture.

Nevertheless, his migration drive persisted, and he climbed back to the treetops, feeling the sun's presence as much as seeing it, following the path of millions of determined robins before him. It was their battle as much as his. For a third time he tried to climb high, scanning the horizon for landmarks. Ahead he saw it. A large, narrow object jutted high into the air. It was a chimney. It looked like the one. But the stack was just barely visible to the robin and certainly would have been impossible for a man to see at that range. Indeed, to the robin it seemed to fade from view and then roll back into his vision, an illusion caused by varying amounts of mist dumped ahead of the bird by the low-hanging clouds. He altered his course slightly, vectoring toward the huge stack. But as he got closer he began to get confused. This couldn't be it. For one thing, an enormous frozen lake of more than five thousand acres lay between him and the chimney. And he did not remember seeing it like that. But he vaguely did recall seeing such a lake on one of his high flights. And then he also remembered seeing another one northeast of that one. He looked toward the northeast, but he couldn't have seen another lake if it was there because of the mist. So, confused because of his apparent closeness—he did remember some of the landmarks—but upset because this wasn't the specific chimney he was looking for, the robin flew on. He flew across the lake, dropping low to skim over the mushy-looking ice and climbing high over steep banks on the northwest corner of the lake. Then he turned slightly to the west to head straight for the huge chimney, even though he knew it was the wrong one.

As he neared it, a brick chimney almost ninety feet tall, he put his tail down, his nose up, and made deeper, harder strokes with his wings. It was a pointless maneuver, but the robin climbed right to the top of the chimney and landed there.

A human would have been discouraged, but a robin's emotions aren't that complex. However, he was tired, very hungry, and confused. It was apparent to him that he was off course. He also knew that he wasn't far from where he wanted to be. He knew that he had once seen the huge lake, which now was about a mile to the southeast of him, but he had seen it only from a distance. The impression that there was another lake near here was indelibly stamped on his brain. It was the fact that he could not see it that confused him.

He looked down and saw a house of glass. It was somewhat like the man houses he had come to know, yet it was strangely different. Behind him the lake had the same gloomy color of the sky, its waters and their potential for reflection hidden by the mushy ice that would remain for at least three more weeks, maybe longer if the days stayed cloudy and chilly. Around him, as far as he could see, were open fields of four main types: plowed fields that were black and muddy-looking; chopped yellow or green fields of corn stubble or alfalfa; pastureland that was still the dark green of winter (but hinting of the brighter green that would come with the sun); and occasional tallgrass marshes with phragmites and cattails where, here and there, a few early-arriving male Red-winged Blackbirds were on guard, protecting their chosen territories, watching the skies for the arrival of the females. They would have to wait almost ten days.

While some of this interested the robin because it looked like good hunting country—and he was hungry—he still felt the strongest drive to press on to find his territory. He sat for almost five minutes because of his fatigue, but then he dove from the stack. He fell almost nose down for twenty yards before finally spreading his wings, leveling off, and resuming his steady, strong flight to the northeast.

His confusion was beginning to get him into trouble. Though he didn't know it, he was only twenty miles west of where he wanted to be. If it had been a bright sunny day he surely would have found his territory. But the mist, and the low flight that it caused, made him miss his landmarks. His drive to migrate pushed him to the northeast, causing him to pass by the territory that destiny had imprinted in his brain.

21

SPRING

ONLY FIVE MINUTES had gone by since the young robin had left the chimney, but he was tiring rapidly. Yet he flew on, because the signals he was getting from inside and outside told him he was near home. Everything below looked right! Well, nearly right. He recognized the landscape, the different kinds of trees—a few elms, maples, oaks, ash, black cherries—trees that represented the kind of place he wanted to be, but this was not the exact place.

His flight was becoming labored. He was tired. He hadn't eaten anything for a long while. And his efforts were complicated by a couple of weather changes now taking place. The wind began to come up, blowing from the northwest and requiring corrections in his course and considerably more effort to fly. Besides that, the mist was becoming scattered and the overcast was intermittently broken as higher clouds and even complete breaks in the cloud cover began to appear. These continual changes in light values were causing disorientation for the robin. He was having difficulty keeping track of the position of the sun, which compounded his confusion and his weariness.

In response, the young robin stopped nearly every hundred yards, landing for a few seconds in a treetop or on a power line, but then pressing on, fighting his fatigue and hunger.

Still, weariness was winning the battle. After each four or five wing beats he closed his wings tight to his body. Typically a robin will open them again in less than one second, but each time now he was tempted to leave them closed because it felt so good. He felt like hurtling to the ground and just sitting. He might have finally done just that had he not seen the cedar thicket ahead of him. It was only a couple of hundred yards away, on the pastured slope that was part of the grounds of a dairy farm.

Cedars made him confident. They would give him food and shelter and this east-facing slope was protected from the northwest wind that was now blowing even harder.

Wearily the young robin dropped low as he approached the hill, flying over a blacktop road, under the power lines that ran along it, just skirting the edge of a couple of small oaks. Then he landed beneath one of the large cedars.

He rested for a few minutes, flew up into the tree and found a few berries, then flew down the hill to some lower-lying land where his experience told him he might expect to find water. He finally did find a puddle, drank his fill, and flew back to the security of the cedars. He found a nice protected branch near the trunk of one of the older trees and in no time at all was dozing off. From time to time during the afternoon he left his perch to feed and drink some more, but after each foray he returned to the cedar to rest and sleep. By late afternoon the sky had almost cleared and the last bits of low-hanging grayness were being pushed out rapidly by the strong northwest wind. Though it got colder with the clear sky, it became more comfortable for him as the wind dried off the dampness that had accumulated everywhere. By now the young robin's breast, back, and wing muscles were exceedingly stiff and sore, and this ache, plus the general fatigue that followed great physical effort, kept him from moving on.

Instead he sat, fluffed up, out of the wind, recovering from the effort that had nearly gotten him home. He felt that he was close. And he also felt an urge to fly high in the clear sky to look for landmarks. Twice that afternoon the urge intensified as he heard the calls of other robins passing overhead, obstructed from his view by the cedar branches. The young robin didn't answer. He remained still and quiet as the sky changed from blue to red, then to pink, dark blue, and finally black. Several times during the night he awoke, cocked his head to look at the bright pinpoints of light twinkling down from the dark, clear sky, and then started to sing his whisper song. He would whisper only a couple of notes, then sit for a few seconds, and finally tuck his beak back under his wing and close his eyes.

• • •

The first light was just beginning to turn the eastern sky light blue with hints of soft pink when the robin was awakened with a start. He heard a noise he dreaded, that made him want to flee, but he instead got so frightened he could not move. As he sat he felt the fear surge through his stiff and tired body, and the minute motion in his tail that the trembling created. It was an oh-so-slight up-and-down movement that could just barely be seen. But it made the robin feel as though he was shaking all over, and he tried even harder to be still.

There it was again! The low-pitched, resonant hunting call of the Great Horned Owl. Although it was a desperate time for most wildlife, nature had chosen early spring for Great Horned Owl young to emerge from their eggs. Thus, when the young owls would be learning how to hunt, the unwise, uneducated young of their prey species would be just learning to be on their own, providing easy hunting as the owls mastered the skills they would need to keep themselves alive.

The owl sounded very near. But even though the robin could see better in the dark than many birds, he could not detect the huge bird of prey. Then, to his left, near the top of the small hill on which the stand of cedars grew, he saw motion. He watched as a spotted skunk walked slowly and hesitantly through the dead grass. It was a female, heavy with young. She was returning to her den, a hole in the ground in the low area near where the robin had bathed the previous afternoon. She was hunting her way back to her den, looking for a mouse or a ground-roosting bird to carry with her to eat in her lair. Her evening hunt had not been successful—she'd caught only a small, sick Horned Lark that was sleeping on the ground near the blacktop and it had not completely satisfied her.

The skunk moseyed along, sticking her nose in every little hole and tuft of grass, her long black tail high in the air. She poked along the top of the hill as the sky got lighter, and worked closer and closer until she was just beneath the young robin's roost in the cedar trees. He had almost forgotten about the owl sound as the light increased and he watched the skunk. But then he saw it. The skunk must have seen it at the same time for she wheeled sharply to turn her rear toward the silent charge of the owl. With her body bent like a hairpin, she raised her tail and aimed her weapons toward the onrushing owl. She discharged her gas into the air and snapped her sharp, needle-like teeth together. But neither the weapon nor the threat deterred the predator. Now falling as much as gliding on half-closed wings, the owl struck, closing its huge talons on the body of the skunk, severing the spinal cord and killing it instantly. The owl's momentum caused both the bird and its prey to roll over, but the owl righted itself and simply sat there, its talons embedded deeply in the skunk. It watched its prey until all movement stopped. Then the owl readjusted its grip and began the process of tearing the skunk open. It would eat part of it and then carry the remainder of the corpse to its two young, perched on a nest of sticks high in a maple tree that grew at the edge of a nearby estate.

After the owl flew off, the robin sat still and quiet. Soon the fear left him, but the energy in his body created by the fear made him nervous and edgy. He flashed his tail open and closed several times and then hopped down four branches of the cedar tree, only to hop back up to where he'd started. Finally, he was no longer afraid to leave the security of the tree, and he flew out and up into the high branches of an oak growing nearby. It was lighter now, too, and this made him feel confident and not as afraid as he had been.

He called out to no bird in particular and everything in general. One long note followed by several shorter notes served as an admonition to the whole world and a warning to other robins that there was trouble in these woods—that it was a good place to avoid. Again he scolded, flashing and bobbing his tail with each note. And finally, at the end of this "lecture," he took his own advice.

He flew up from the limb, calling twice to any others of his kind that might be near. Then he climbed into the eastern sky, flying to meet the sun, climbing high to look for landmarks that would be easy to see on a clear sky. Flying was easy today in spite of the stiffness in his muscles. And his urge to move was even stronger than his morning hunger. In a couple of minutes he had climbed to nearly two hundred feet. Behind him the sun cast long shadows that stretched to the west. To the south he saw the lake, its bluish ice glistening in the light. This was what he needed. To the northeast he saw another ice-bound lake. This was a lake he remembered.

Though he had never been on this side of it before, he recognized the outline of its northern shore as a place he'd seen from time to time last summer when returning from the roosting areas to his parents' territory. And he remembered its western bay, where he had paused on his fall migration. So he turned even more toward the east and began to scan the horizon for other landmarks.

In a couple of minutes he saw the cattails and reeds that grew along the east end of the lake, where the creek flowed from it through the maze of marshes. He recognized that! And then he saw the water tower that stood east of the chimney. And there, in the distance, was the huge chimney itself, jutting up into the sky on the horizon to the south.

He called out and turned again, flying as fast as he had ever flown in his life. He headed straight for the chimney, and as he got closer he saw other familiar sights. The trees a few miles north and west of the chimney where he had been raised, with the houses, so visible now without leaves on the trees. To the south and west stretched the fast-flowing creek that was a good guideline for getting from the chimney to the roosting grounds along the river. To the east he saw another water tower and the vast open areas of the golf course, just becoming green, probably a highly sought territory for robins.

And straight ahead were the chimney, the brown brick buildings, and the vast expanses of lawn landscaped with evergreens, ash, oak, and maple trees, and shrubs of many kinds.

Straight ahead was home.

22

SPRING

A DARK GREEN SEDAN pulled into a parking lot at the back of the sanatorium's administration building. The two middle-aged men who got out had been on the early shift all winter, starting work at six a.m. to make certain that the main sidewalks and steps were clear of snow and ice. But today, the last Friday in March, would be the end of that shift, for it seemed that spring was here at last.

"Hey, listen to that, Charlie," said one of the men.

"Well, I'll be danged," said Charlie. "I'll be danged! I was beginning to wonder if we was going to hear any robins this year. Now I know spring is here."

"Look. There he is. Sitting on that wire and giving everybody blazes. Look at that pretty red breast of his."

"Yep, that's nice."

Both men smiled and went inside to get ready for another day's work.

The young robin was overwhelmed with energy. Though he was still stiff from the day before and though he had not yet eaten, he was intent on reacquainting himself with his old haunts. He flew through the grounds of the sanatorium, resting on the topmost branches of trees or in the open on telephone wires, continually scolding and calling other robins. His calls weren't greetings, however, or the familiar flock calls. He was challenging. But since he was a first-year robin, operating on his inner feelings and inherited memory, with no experience, he didn't quite know how to go about getting started. First he looked over the grounds. He hadn't picked out exactly where his territory would be, though he somehow knew that he would make his home in the vicinity of the chimney. So he spent the first couple of hours flying from spot to spot, calling, but not singing or marking his territory. He was figuring out the boundaries.

Gradually, after checking out the whole area, he wandered back to the vicinity of the parking lot, which seemed to please him. The land to the south of the parking lot dropped away in a steep decline that leveled out onto a large, shaded lawn. The lawn sloped at its west end into a kind of gully overgrown with a tangle of various shrubs and vines, including viburnum, grape, and Virginia creeper and some poison ivy too. On the other side of the parking lot the land rose steeply and was thickly wooded with a variety of trees and a dense understory. It was not good robin territory at all and not likely to be claimed by any robin. To the east stood the three-story administration building, an unnatural barrier but one that would affect robin territories (unlike homes, which are part of a territory, or may even be divided in half, with one robin's territory taking in part of a home, and another robin's the other part).

Beyond the gully, the lawn started again and ran nearly a quarter of a mile up to a tarred road. The lawn was liberally landscaped with ash, oak, and maple trees and had numerous shrubbery beds of barberry, honeysuckle, and lilac. It was excellent breeding habitat for robins and far more territory than the robin could ever defend.

Several times during his first day he flew to other areas on the grounds, but he always returned to this spot near the administration building. He hunted on the lawns, drank and bathed in both the puddles in the parking lots and those in the bottom of the gully, and sat and preened on several high spots that gave him a good view of the territory that he was defining in his mind.

Though he scolded a couple of times and called out challenges as he landed on each perch, he sang only parts of songs, and did that only a couple of times. Gradually the idea began to form in his mind that the half acre of ground and trees he had been watching was his. So he began to look for other robins—other male robins—that might intrude. What he didn't know was that other male robins returning daily to claim other territories in the northland were possessed with the same territorial drive.

As the sun began to set against the barren branches that marked the horizon in this spot, the young robin glided from his perch on the telephone wire just at the edge of the parking lot. He dropped rapidly to a puddle that sat in a depression in the lot, drank deeply of its cold water (which would be ice before morning), and bathed energetically. Then he flew to a horizontal branch in an ash tree growing near the door of the administration building, where he preened, carefully drying and arranging his feathers, working especially hard on his breast feathers and the long tertial feathers where the wing and back came together.

Then, when the sun set and pink twilight streaked the spring sky, the young robin flew with slow, jerky strokes of his wings and flashing of his tail to the high wooden pole that supported the power lines above the parking lot. From the top of the pole he looked out over his territory and began to sing. His first few notes were soft and hesitant, but each subsequent note was louder until within a few seconds he was singing with all his power, drawing in deep breaths and quivering his tail at the end of every phrase. As he sang he looked down on this land that he called his own, and the sight of it filled him with the emotion of possession. He looked around at it, at the maples and oaks, the honeysuckles, even the puddles, unconsciously memorizing every one from every angle. Then, abruptly, in the middle of a phrase, he stopped, dropped from his perch, and glided quietly into the branches of the large spruce that stood at the far corner of the big brick building. He hopped about, found a perch that seemed safe and comfortable, fluffed up his feathers, stuck his beak under his wing, and went to sleep.

His songs would be longer when there were other robins to hear them.

At Worthington, Minnesota, the next day, a twin-engine Cessna was forced to veer from its final approach into the Worthington Airport. The reason was that a cloud of ducks, about ten thousand Mallards and Pintails, was circling and milling about the airspace that man had reserved for the airplanes. The pilot saw the birds and knew that a collision could be fatal.

That same morning on a farm in the Delmarva Peninsula of Maryland, a forty-four-year-old poultry farmer and bird-watcher was looking over his favorite waterfowl resting areas on Chesapeake Bay. "Darn. They're gone," he said to no one in particular. "The geese are gone." Every year the retreat of the Canada Geese back to their breeding grounds east of Hudson's Bay left the man filled with a fleeting melancholy. He knew that the departure of the geese would be followed by arrivals of new birds that would delight him. But there was something especially wild about the call of the geese. He smiled, turned his head to one side, and faced a grove of pine trees and oaks that someone had planted years ago. A robin was singing loudly from the top of one of the closer trees. The man looked at it through his binoculars, smiled again, and started to walk back through the tall grass to the dirt road where he had parked his car.

"Right you are, fella. It's spring," he said, and he began to whistle. The young robin did not see another robin all the next day. But twice, faintly, he heard a robin's song coming from somewhere beyond the far side of the heavily wooded hill that rose to the north of the parking lot. Once, curious, the young robin flew to the top of the hill, where he called for a couple of minutes. There was no response and he could not see any movement. So he flew back down to the lawn that he had claimed for himself and hunted for insects, which were increasing rapidly in numbers with the advent of regular fifty- and sixty-degree daytime temperatures. His routine that day was the same, a few brief snatches of song, some patrolling of the perimeter of his territory, and then a silent flight to the spruce tree for his evening sleep.

The next day dawn came abruptly because of low, thick clouds that blocked off the predawn light. When it finally did brighten, enormous flakes of wet snow melted on the warm ground and seemed to have a quieting effect on the animals and birds. The young robin remained in the spruce for nearly half an hour after waking and then decided to try and find some fruit. His experience with this kind of weather told him that insects would be hard to find. But finding fruit meant leaving his territory.

He burst decisively from the spruce tree, using deep, powerful wing beats to wind and twist through the treetops. In a few seconds he flew beyond the western boundary of his territory, toward some houses on the far side of the road that marked the edge of the sanatorium property. As he got to the road he stopped, called a couple of times, and looked for fruit-bearing trees, or at least a promising tangle. He saw neither. Then a movement about 150 yards north caught his eye. It was another robin, winging through the tops of distant trees. Suddenly it landed, flashed its tail, and called out. Instantly, the young robin answered and in the same breath darted out of the tree, turning north to pursue the other robin, the first of his kind he had seen so close since he left his traveling companion in the farmyard. But the bird he sought suddenly dove, plummeting behind a house, out of the young robin's sight.

Only three houses separated the robin from where the other bird disappeared, but suddenly the young robin felt uneasy and afraid. Abruptly he swerved to his left and landed on a television antenna attached to the side of a brick chimney.

He called out twice, expecting an answer from the other bird, but he heard no sound except the slight fluttering of limbs caused by the gentle

----

easterly breeze. Hesitantly, the young robin flew from the chimney in a slow, controlled pattern that would enable him to turn and flee immediately if something should happen. He passed over the house, then glided silently to the peak of the next house's roof. There he saw it.

Just past the gray-and-white asphalt shingles the young robin could see the topmost branches of a small tree. On those branches hung hundreds of reddish-brown fruits. The fruits looked a lot like the hawthorns that the young robin was familiar with, but they also looked like very tiny apples. He ran down the roof to its edge and then spread his wings to glide into the branches of the tree, a flowering crab apple of a variety that holds its fruit through the winter.

Fluttering his wings, he edged out onto one of the branches at the top of the tree, tugged a couple of times at the fruit, broke it free from the stem, and swallowed it whole in two big gulps. Swallowing it was hard because of its size, but it tasted good and pleased him.

So he looked for another one and reached to it, extending his body as far as he could and tugging it off the stem with sharp backward jerks of his head, not unlike the moves he used to pull an earthworm from its hole. Then he dropped it. He sat for a second, looking down at the fallen fruit. The impulse came to just take another one. But instead of doing that he dropped from the branch, nose down, and dove toward the earth, swooping to break his fall with open wings and tail just above the ground. He had to take a couple of steps to get to the fruit, but he quickly picked it up with his beak, tipped his head back to open his throat, and swallowed it.

Then, all of a sudden, pandemonium! The young robin saw the other bird coming at him, recognized it as another robin, and knew by the posture of the oncoming attacker that he had violated its territory. The young robin ducked low to the ground, wheeled to present his beak to the attacking male, lowered his head, and snapped at the oncoming bird. But the attacker hit the young robin's neck with his foot, and the blow hurt. While the young robin did like crab apples, there was something in this other bird's demeanor that made him know he couldn't win a fight here. He needed to flee back to the security of his own territory.

He flew, climbing along the back of the house and turning sharply at its edge to reach treetop height. The attacking robin followed him for about thirty yards and then quit, landing on a tree branch, flashing his tail and scolding loudly. The feathers on his head and the back of his neck stood out as visible signs of his anger.

The young robin retraced his route over the two houses, but when he saw the parking lot, he angled back across the trees to his territory. When he got there he flew to one of his favorite resting perches, a broad horizontal limb in an old oak tree. From this branch he could watch his entire territory while remaining somewhat protected from above and behind. The tree, probably seventy years old, was about twenty yards from the building. The area behind it was wide open because of the parking lot. And the tree stood on high ground that gave the young robin a vantage point that was almost as good as when he perched on the power line that ran along the edge of the parking lot.

He wasn't too upset about having lost the first real fight of the spring. After all, he wasn't protecting anything. But his neck was sore from the blow he had received. And the weather was still bad, snowing and misting. It was simply the kind of day for doing a lot of sitting, watching, and waiting.

23

SPRING

As the days passed, he began to get neighbors. In less than a week several male robins claimed territories nearby, the first on the west, then others to the south near his roosting spruce, then to the east, on the other side of the administration building.

One even claimed the wooded hill behind the parking lot for a couple of days but soon gave up the territory and moved on. It was not a good place to find food in the robin style.

The influx of competitors made life almost unbearably tense for the young male. One challenger or another was always running or flying into his territory. It nearly drove him crazy. He felt that he had to spend all his time watching over his grounds. He had to hurry his bath and interrupt feeding and preening at the most inopportune moments.

He had taken up his old routine of flying to the drippy faucet near the storage building to drink and bathe, and this habit nearly always led to two confrontations. The faucet was about two hundred yards from the territory the robin had selected. In order to get there he had to trespass on the territories of three other male robins. He soon learned, however, that if he climbed beyond treetop height he could cross these territories without being challenged. In other words, territorial boundaries extended up, but only so far. So whenever he flew nearer to the ground, he was chased. And he always flew near the ground for the last thirty yards, which almost always led to a skirmish.

Wouldn't you know it? An ambitious two-year-old male had attempted to claim the drippy faucet and puddle as part of his territory, even though it was a good thirty yards from the nearest tree and absolutely worthless as a hunting ground. The problem the two-year-old had was that while he was trying to drive one robin from this remote part of his claim, another would usually move onto another part. The other part, of course, was more desirable to the two-year-old, so he would forsake the faucet area temporarily to drive off the other intruder. The fact was he had simply bitten off more than he could chew, and he was doing a lousy job of defending the territory he was trying to claim. He would eventually have to give up some of it.

Nevertheless, for the time being, the young robin's bath was usually interrupted by a skirmish. First would be the chase by another first-year male as the robin began descending from the treetops to the puddle. This was noisy but short-lived, and it rarely resulted in any contact. The problem was that the first bird's scolding alerted the two-year-old, and no matter what he was doing, he would fly to a tree to see what the fuss was about.

Meanwhile, the young robin would land, walk into the puddle, take a couple of drinks, and usually begin bathing only seconds before the two-year-old arrived. While it is true that robins like water, they don't like to fight in it. Thus the older bird would stand at the edge of the pond for a couple of seconds, weaving his head, jabbing and clicking his beak to threaten the young robin. Though the young robin would continue his bath, he wasn't calm and cool about it. He rushed because he didn't want to fight in the water either. And the young robin knew that he was the intruder no matter how weak the two-year-old's claim was, and that therefore he would probably lose the fight. Besides, he didn't want to fight for the spot as much as the older bird did. Especially when he was wet. But then, almost every time, just as a physical confrontation was near, the older bird would see an intruder elsewhere in his territory and rush back, leaving the young robin wet and agitated but relieved.

Usually the young robin would then fly another thirty yards to a power line that ran under the eave of the storage shed. It was a safe, protected site for post-bath preening and, happily for him, it was not part of any other robin's territory. After a quick preening and oiling session, the young robin would hurry home to defend his territory.

He first saw her after spending one week alone. It was about ten thirty on a bright, shining morning. His day had been typical so far: some song in the early morning, a worm-and-bug hunt that was quite successful, a patrol of the perimeters of his territory—marking them with song, and then a quick drink from a puddle in the gully. He had almost finished preening himself in an aspen sapling and was about to fly to his observation post in the oak when he saw her.

It wasn't a male.

He knew that as soon as he saw her. The difference made his heart pound with excitement. The female was hunting on the lawn at the far south end of his territory. She was smaller than he was. Her head was lighter than his, her breast not so red, her back colored more toward the brown shades than his. She too was in her first breeding season, though he couldn't know that, and she was not alone. Just beyond her but still in the young male's territory, was another male robin. It was not the male who usually intruded there, the one whose territory lay just to the south of the young robin's. It was a stranger, a year older than he was.

The young robin bounded out of the aspen tree and flew toward the birds in a slow, cautious flight that was marked by much tail flashing and exaggerated wing beats. At his approach the strange male ducked his head and opened his beak.

The young robin, cautious and inexperienced, afraid and unsure of what to do, landed about five feet from the two birds. He immediately ran in a course that was parallel to his boundary line. He wanted to fight the strange male, but competing with that impulse was his need to watch the female, to sing to her and to run before her so she could see how strong and capable he was. His lack of experience showed in that he could not anticipate what she would do.

The young robin stopped and watched the female. He felt a need to express that this was his territory and to indicate his excitement, his eagerness to have her, and his willingness to fight for her. Rather than a song that came from his throat, he poured out a mixture of calls and threats, and right in the middle of this confusion came a high-pitched but soft song. It was truly a reflection of his excitement at this moment and his mixed feelings at seeing both an unmated female and a competitor in his territory.

He began to run again, moving parallel to his territorial boundary. In response to this move the strange male challenged the young robin by running toward him, putting himself between the young male and the female. In an instant the young male wheeled around and charged the stranger. He expected the strange bird to flee as his neighbors did when they intruded on his territory. Instead, the intruder stabbed at the young robin with his beak, determined to fight. The young robin stopped just inches from the older bird, faced him directly, and then jumped into him, striking him in the breast with his breast muscles. He leaped high enough to pass his head over the strange male's head and struck at him with his beak. The stranger countered, trying to jump higher than the young robin, but the young robin anticipated the move. He jumped up, fluttering his wings, and again exceeded the stranger's highest leap. Adding injury to insult, he came down on one side of the stranger and struck him in the neck with his beak.

Twisting hard to his right, the stranger struck back at the young robin and then ran sideways for two feet. It may have been an attempt to get away, but to the young robin it was an insult because it took the stranger farther into the young robin's territory. Quickly he flew at the bird. The stranger turned again to meet him, and both birds, in a spectacular effort to attain psychological supremacy, slammed their breasts together in a violent collision and then leaped and flew straight up into the air, still bumping each other. With a fluttering, wrestling motion the contesting robins climbed twelve feet. Still hitting. Still trying to outdo each other. Then the young male gained the advantage. Perhaps it was a gust of wind. Perhaps it was his own strength. But he felt the strange bird's center of gravity shift slightly backward, putting the young robin in a position from which he could exert downward pressure to force the older bird down. And that was what he did. The moment he felt the stranger tip backward, the young robin closed his wings and rode him down to the ground. They crashed with a thump that was loud to them and painful to the strange robin, mostly because of the force of the young robin falling on him. He cried out. It was a loud sound that the young robin had never heard before, but one that he understood perfectly.

Immediately the strange robin turned and fled, and the young robin flew after him in a showy, flashy flight with spreading tail and slow, full strokes of his wings. The young bird scolded the other male as he fled, then landed for an instant on the ground at the edge of his territory, then turned once again to make the acquaintance of the young female.

She was waiting near the spot where he had first seen her. At his approach she began to run along the lawn, hunting. The young male landed about six feet from her and hunted there, staying near her. He picked up a bug here and there, occasionally sang in his soft whisper voice, and by his motions encouraged her to stay within the boundaries of his territory.

Together they explored his territory this way, with the male leading and directing her by his position. Subtle movements of his head and changes in his posture helped her learn in robin language the boundaries of this bountiful land he wanted to share. Occasionally they would begin to fly to another spot to hunt or just rest, but when he thought she was going to leave the territory that he had claimed he would fly in front of her and then land on the ground or in a low tree or bush, marking the boundary with calls, actions, and posture.

In a few minutes she had a clear understanding of what the young male was offering her. If it appealed to her instincts and her inherited and real memories, she would stay. If it didn't, she would leave.

Once, while they were hunting, she headed off in the direction of the gully and began to fly toward the west, beyond his territory, but he went after her. In less than thirty yards he overtook her, and when he stopped in a small oak she stopped too. Just as they had landed, the male claiming that territory moved in and challenged the young robin, attempting to get between the young male and his prospective mate.

When this challenger tried this technique, the female turned back toward the young male's territory, flying at great speed. The young robin flew after her as fast as he could, and the other male chased them both to the territory boundary, scolding and fussing all the way.

For the rest of the day they stayed within each other's sight. Not that they were always close. Sometimes he would be in a tree preening and she would be on the ground at the other end of the territory hunting. But each knew where the other was, and as the afternoon passed, they often hunted within ten yards of each other.

That evening, as she hunted on the ground, the young robin flew to the top of the telephone pole near the parking lot and sang loudly. And as she was hunting below he saw another male fly into their territory about two feet above the ground. Before he could leave his perch on the pole to drive the intruder away, the female turned and dove at the trespasser herself, frightening him off with the seriousness of her threat and the noisy calls she made.

After her attack, she followed the intruder to the boundary by the gully and sat and scolded for a few moments before resuming her hunt for a snack before sleeping.

Now she had demonstrated that she claimed it as her territory, too.

24

SPRING

H E DIDN'T KNOW what the young female was up to. But whatever it was, it excited him and caused him to follow her everywhere. They had been together for a week, but it was only yesterday afternoon that she began this strange behavior.

He had to follow her.

At the moment she was in one of the few remaining elms, a ten-year-old tree growing very close to the edge of the gully. She flew to a branch just at the point where it split off from the thin trunk. At first she sat there for a few minutes looking puzzled, as if pondering her next move. He, of course, was near her, sitting above her in the tree and watching everything she did while also looking over his territory for intruders or danger. The young female then half walked and half flew out from the trunk toward the tip of the branch. After a couple of feet she came to a place where the branch forked. There she stopped and squatted.

Her body rocked from side to side as she tucked her legs up into her belly. As she nestled down into the crotch she tipped her head back and her beak up slightly. It was this movement, this posture that excited the young male.

But then she abruptly got up and moved farther out on the branch, just as she had done so many times before this day, squirming and squatting on every likely spot. When she got to the end of the branch, he expected her to fly to another. Instead she flew back to the first place and tried it again. Finally she sat there for a few minutes without moving or squirming, just resting and relaxing in that strange, exciting posture.

The young male might have guessed that this was coming. He and his mate had both seen the other robins near their territory doing the same thing. In fact, witnessing this activity seemed to increase their own excitement level and had a large part in inspiring the young female to start surveying tree limbs for suitable nesting spots. While it was true that her instinctive memory would have a great deal to do with the type of nest she would build, she was a natural mimic, like most birds, and very aware of the actions of others of her species that were occupying surrounding territories.

Thus, while her emotions made her anxious and eager to do something, it helped her know exactly what to do when she saw the female that lived to the south nestle down into the crotch of a flowering crab apple tree.

(This is not to say that a female robin living isolated in the woods someplace wouldn't know how to build a nest. Through trial and error she would ultimately strike upon the correct set of actions that would satisfy her nervousness and her need to nestle into tree crotches. Learning simply came faster to the young female because of the opportunity to watch another.)

As if dissatisfied, the young female flew to the top of the tree, leaving the crotch with a strong jump and quick, deep strokes of her wings. When she got to the top she explored several of the higher branches of the elm. But they were probably too flimsy. After a few minutes she returned to the fork of the branch on the lower limb. It seemed right to her for reasons that she couldn't understand or even wonder about. It simply was the most satisfying place.

Since the tree grew by the gully, it had not received the careful pruning of most of the trees on the sanatorium grounds. That was why its lower branches were still intact.

The branch on which she rested was the first horizontal branch jutting out from the tree and was only about seven feet off the ground. However, since it grew out over the gully, where the ground dropped away, the crotch was almost twenty feet above the gully's bottom, directly below.

It was a peculiar-looking branch. That was because the site she selected was the result of breakage of the branch years earlier, when it was forming. The branch actually dropped down to the spot where the nest would be built, and then, at that fork, both halves of the branch grew nearly vertically in the air. The two upshooting branches that created the fork were much younger than the main branch. It would be a nice secure spot that could hold a well-fashioned nest.

For several minutes the young female sat gazing through the branches, which still did not have leaves. Once her mate started to sing. His voice and song excited her and made her heart beat faster. Then suddenly she flew down to the lawn to hunt. She was hungry.

The young male robin remained at his perch on the tree for a few minutes, watching his mate and overlooking their territory. Then he glided down toward her, landing with a run about ten feet from where she stood. Just as he arrived, she stooped low, moved her body away from him somewhat, and looked at him over her shoulder. She squatted a little lower and began to flutter her wings, much like a juvenile bird begging for food. Her actions deeply excited and aroused the young male. He ran to her and mounted her, and this brief but intense act of copulation made him feel the same emotions that he felt when singing or when he saw her crouched in the fork of the tree, only the feeling now was stronger and much more intense. She, too, responded to his touch, and the link between them grew even stronger at that moment.

The next morning they mated again several times, and that day the young female began building the first nest she had ever built in her life.

After his morning song and a skirmish caused by an attempted intrusion of their territory by the robin to the south, the young male began to follow his mate. And that was when he knew something new was about to happen. At first it was the same feeling, an emotional sensation when he saw her pick up some dead grass in her beak. But she quickly dropped it and resumed her hunt for worms and bugs at the edge of the gully, where tall grass grew next to the lawn and long strands of dead grass lay in profusion. He hunted near her and watched her curiously. After she had tugged a couple more worms from the ground, she ran again to the edge of the lawn and picked up several strands of grass in her beak. Again he felt the emotion and watched as she flew to the crotch of the tree, sat for a couple of minutes, and then dropped the grass. It blew away. Her inexperience was obvious. She really didn't know what to do. She was just figuring it out.

Briskly, with fast, broken flight, she dropped back down to the edge of the lawn and picked up another load of grass. This time, as she flew toward the nest site, the young male followed along, landing on another branch ten feet higher than the nest site. From there he watched his mate drop the grass again, only to see it blow away. Puzzled and confused, she returned to the lawn to pick up more. Instead of following her, the young male remained on his perch. This time he watched as she picked up some grass and then dropped it onto the ground after running a couple of feet. Then she flew into the low branches of a small aspen sapling, where she sat for nearly half a minute, looking this way and that. Then, almost as if to say, "Aha," she pushed off the branch in direct and purposeful flight toward the brush pile where she had occasionally roosted. There, a couple of years before, a maintenance crew had piled debris from two small trees that had blown down in a summer storm. With the trees (which had been cut into easily handled pieces) had been piled various limbs from other pruning and grooming jobs, and the result was an enormous pile, about twelve feet in diameter and nearly eight feet high. The men had tossed it into the gully to slow the runoff of water and erosion. It also proved to be a tremendous resource for birds and other wildlife, providing shelter, a roosting site, and nesting cover.

Since she had slept there several times, the young female was very familiar with it and the trickle of water that so often flowed down the gully and finally oozed under the pile. It was the water flow that drew her. She landed first in a sapling to look for possible danger. Then she glided down past the base of the brush pile to a puddle. The water flowed from a culvert that drained the parking lot on the hill far above. The brush pile effectively slowed the flow of the water, making a muddy puddle about six inches long and a foot wide. It wasn't much, but at the sight of it the young female knew exactly what to do. She picked up some of the grass that lay near the mud in her beak. Then she stuck her beak into the mud at the edge of the puddle, mud that was not gooey but that had a cookie-dough consistency. Then she turned and flew with the material up the gully, terminating her flight with a nearly vertical climb to the nest site. She landed about a foot from the spot, looked the area over for possible danger, then hopped along the branch. When she got to the crotch, she stuck her head down and deposited the gooey glob at its base. Then she squatted on it and turned around a couple of times, packing the material down into the coarse bark with her feet and breast.

She repeated her trip again and again, working throughout the entire morning, building the base of the cup to about an inch and a half high. Twice during that time the young male followed her down to the muddy spot, and once he actually picked up a strand of grass. But it was more in mimicry of her than in a desire to assist. Twice he followed her to the branch where the nest was taking form and as a result of that, and his emotional excitement with what she was doing, the nesting site assumed a great deal of importance in his scheme of things.

However, at other times while she was building it, he would hunt or simply sit and rest at one of his many favorite spots in the territory.

Several times during the morning she took a break from nest building to feed and bathe. But as soon as she came back from the dripping faucet or the parking lot puddle, cleaned up and well groomed, she would go back to the mud and get dirty all over again.

By two o'clock in the afternoon she was fatigued. Sore and aching, her muscles especially tired from the climbing flights carrying the mud, the young female stopped for the day. She spent nearly twenty minutes hunting on the lawn, flew to the dripping faucet to bathe again, and returned to her territory. There she and her mate loafed away the balance of the day, hunting and resting. It was as if they had forgotten about the nest site.

But the next morning, after the song period, some exercise flights, hunting, and an attempt to intrude upon the territory to the east, the female went back to work. Again the male watched her labor. Even though he was often hunting or preening quite far from her, he always watched her and what she was doing. Today he also sang to her while she was working, singing loudly from the boundaries of his territory and singing both loud and soft songs from the upper branches of the elm tree where the nest was taking form. His song inspired and encouraged her. It helped keep the link between them strong and helped bring the nesting site into the center of their emotional bond. It was as if the site became the product of their union, so strong was their attachment to it.

The weather remained warm and pleasant. Although the lack of precipitation threatened to dry up her source of mud, the female kept busy at her task for three more days. Her efforts left her very weary toward the end of each day, but she was increasingly driven by an inner urgency, a need to complete the rounded cup of mud and grass, shaped by her breast and body, and the need to lay her eggs there.

She had never laid an egg before, or even seen one, for that matter, but somehow she knew that something was forming inside her and she knew she would have to deposit it in the nest she was making.

Finally, at about noon on the fifth day of labor, the nest was done. She knew her work was finished. It was just the right height to hold her snugly. It had just the right hardness to make it feel safe and secure to her, and it was soft inside. She snuggled down into the nest once, slowly worked her way out, looked in again, and then flew off, calling loudly to her mate.

Twisting and turning through the branches, she flew down the gully, turning with a flair and a rush of wind through her wings to fly parallel along the southern boundary of her territory.

From his perch on the wire by the parking lot the young male flew to join his mate, who was flying the slow, deliberate, flashing flight of a robin that is about to land. But she went on, surprising him, and penetrated into the territory of the robin to the south. Quickly that male flew to intercept her, scolding all the while. But she quickly climbed away from him, rose beyond the trees, and headed across the sanatorium grounds to the dripping faucet to bathe.

After a vigorous bath and preening, followed by a leisurely flight back above the treetops, the young female returned to the territory and beckoned to her mate to copulate with her. Then both birds spent the rest of the day feeding, preening, and enjoying the warmth of the April sun.

At the next dawn, as her mate was singing from atop the parking lot pole, the young female quietly flew to the nest, snuggled down into it for fifteen minutes, and laid a single bluish-green egg. The sensation was somewhat painful but at the same time strangely pleasant to the young bird. And when she felt it was time to go, she stood up slowly on the rim of the nest and looked back into it for a minute, staring at the nest she had constructed and the egg that had caused her both pain and pleasure. The sight of it created a different but equally strong sensation in her. She felt a need to protect it, to snuggle in on it. But she also felt a need to leave the nest, a desire to ignore it. Finally that feeling won, and she flew from the nest, never to return that day.

But though she didn't go to it, she watched it from a distance, and once even charged a large male grackle that had landed on the ground below it. The young male, too, joined in this chase and shared his mate's strong protectiveness about this spot and the nest that she had built.

"Hey, Charlie, I saw that robin that's been hanging out around the admin building and his mate in a heckuva fight today."

"With what?" asked Charlie, as he washed his hands at the end of his shift.

"Oh, they were chasin' an old blackbird away from the gully. I'll bet you a dollar they got their nest down there somewheres."

"Yeah," said Charlie. "They probably do. I think a robin can handle those big old blackbirds. It's those jays I worry about."

"There's not much we can do about it," said Charlie's friend, "except wish 'em luck."

"You're right there. C'mon, let's go home."

SPRING

A CLOUDY DAWN FOR the first time in a week greeted the pair of robins, and the falling barometer and the restlessness it created caused the young male to sing loudly throughout the morning. With the dawn came a gentle mist that slowly turned to a slight drizzle as the morning temperature rose.

The idea of moisture was both good and bad for the young female. She knew that hunting would be good that day, but she also had to keep her eggs dry. That morning, after she had deposited her last egg, she remained on the nest and seemed content to do so. Partly because of the rain, and partly because of the new emotion overtaking her, the young female sat on the nest much longer than the ten minutes she ordinarily spent. Perhaps that was what caused the trouble. Perhaps it would have happened anyway.

Far down at the end of the gully, near where it entered a cement culvert and ran under the road, another nest was being built. It was only about six feet off the ground, in the fork of a box elder sapling that had sprouted amid a tangle of sumac. The nest, a skillfully woven cup of coarse grasses, was empty. But the mother, who would be laying eggs soon, had a strong need for protein. While she was an energetic and very self-sufficient bird, she was not the bug-and-worm hunter that the robin was—for one thing, she simply didn't know how to pull a worm out of the ground.

But she was a Blue Jay. Like all jays, she was resourceful and able to make up for a lack of specialization by cunning, furtiveness, and adaptability. She would get the protein her body craved so that she could lay her eggs in the nest.

Partly because of their lack of specialization, Blue Jays occupy considerably more territory per pair than robins do. This jay and her mate had claimed nearly ten acres of the sanatorium grounds and the wooded wetlands to the south. They often didn't hunt close to their own nest, choosing instead to be quiet and obscure. But this day the female had noticed something peculiar up the gully from her nest, and she was moving to see what it was.

The female robin saw her coming, flying short little hops of five to ten yards, then stopping for a couple of seconds before continuing. The sight of the jay immediately angered and frightened the young female, but she sat still, hoping in her fear that the jay would not see her. The young male robin, meanwhile, had stopped singing and was hunting on the asphalt at the edge of the parking lot, looking for worms washed down by the drizzle. From where he stood, because of the log barrier at the edge of the lot, he could see neither the nest nor the approaching jay.

A cardinal was singing in the gully not far from its nest, and the sight of the jay caused it to quit whistling and just sit and watch. But the jay paid no attention to the cardinal. And she could not see the singer's light brown mate hidden on her nest almost at the top of a five-foot-high arborvitae in the middle of the gully.

Instead the jay sneaked farther along toward the robin, sitting so open and exposed on her nest in a tree that still did not have much of a leaf cover. The jay was acting as if she didn't see the female, for she looked here and there as if hunting for bugs or nuts, never looking directly at the nest. The young robin watched the blue jay's eyes, wondering if she had been detected, afraid, yet hoping that her ruse was working. After all, she did kind of resemble a knot on a tree. But though the leaf buds had begun to unfold, the nest was still exposed. To an experienced jay, the silhouette of a robin on the nest, with bill and tail tilting out at slight angles to the sky, was unmistakable. What the jay was trying to determine was whether she should try to get at the nest with the female sitting on it or just hang around until the robin left. She was about ten yards from the nest, undecided, when the robin made her mistake.

Nervous, afraid that she had been detected, the robin trembled and then, to her own astonishment, let out a small, soft, nervous call—four quick low tones.

Surprised by the unexpected sound, the jay turned one bright black eye right at the robin and in that instant the robin knew what the jay was after. She leaped off the nest and plummeted over the side with wings closed and tail up. In the same instant she called out to her mate and scolded the

---

jay in a loud, trembling tone that told every robin within hearing distance that a nest was threatened.

The jay moved quickly to her left to avoid the diving attack and then saw the young male racing toward her, screaming in a frenzy of anger and distress. The jay flew up to the nest with quick, sure strokes. She had to duck her head to avoid the dive and the snapping beak of the female robin. And just as she was about to pick up an egg, the male robin slammed into her with a force that knocked her off the limb. But his momentum made him pass by her, and the jay regained her footing on the cup of the nest with a couple of flaps of her wings. This time she reached her head down quickly and skillfully poked her beak into one of the bright blue eggs, sticking her head into the air to drain and swallow as much of the contents as she could get. The robins, meanwhile, were poised outside the jay's reach, scolding, snapping their beaks in anger and flashing their tails. Other robins had flown off the ground into the trees and were watching with apprehension and anger. Some approached to scold the jay, ignoring the territorial boundaries. But the deed was done, and the robins knew it. Though they were upset, their anger had lost its urgency. In another couple of seconds the jay reached down, popped another egg, thrust her head into the air to swallow the contents, and then pushed off the nest, eager to fly away from the noise and scolding of the angry robins.

They chased the jay to the end of their territory, but the jay slipped through the trees and headed to some tall pines that grew far beyond the territories of all the robins upset by the ruckus.

For several minutes the birds sat and scolded. On that drizzly, dreary morning they repeatedly flew back to the nest site and looked again and again at the broken remnants of their first attempt, as if disbelieving that it had happened. But the finality of the event became a fact in their minds and hearts and by nightfall they ignored the spot, almost as if pretending that they had never even had a nest there. There is no survival benefit in dwelling on a tragedy. Though the birds had undergone considerable trauma and did not sing or mate with each other that day, they would recover.

It was nature's way that the Blue Jays would get their protein from the worms they couldn't hunt by using the robins as middlemen. But there have always been jays and robins. And there probably always will be. At least for as long as it matters.

26

SPRING

NEARLY A WEEK and a half had passed since the Blue Jay had frightened the young robin's mate off her nest and popped the pair's eggs. But to the young robin, it might as well have been a hundred years ago. The thought of the event was gone from his memory (though his wariness of Blue Jays had been permanently heightened). Instead, his attention was focused on his mate.

She sat in a spot visible to him but well concealed from the eyes of most of the birds around them. This time she had built her nest eighteen feet high in the same tall spruce tree that had served him so well as a roosting spot. The spruce's stiff, dense needles protected the nest well from the eyes of intruding jays and grackles. Further protection was afforded by the fact that the tree grew near the brick wall of the administration building, which shielded the tree from the east and keeping it out of the flight paths of most of the area birds. For the nest-robbing species, opportunity is as much a matter of fate as of skill. Thus, by avoiding their most frequently used flight lanes, the robins reduced their odds for a chance exposure of the nest.

The robins still dreaded, and hated, encounters with jays and chased them every time the blue marauders came into their territory. And several times while the new nest was being constructed they heard the pitiful, terrifying calls as other robins fought, and usually lost, battles with jays. But the young robins did not suffer the trauma and grief of continually remembering the emotions they had experienced when they fought their battle. Nevertheless, they were more belligerent toward jays and more apt to notice them when they were near.

It was not a jay but another bird that puzzled the young female during her egg laying. Each night she chose to roost away from the nest in the brush pile in the gully. In the morning, after feeding and drinking, she would fly to the nest in the predawn light, quickly lay an egg, and then fly off the nest, remaining away from it for the rest of the day. The third day, as she flew toward the spruce to lay her egg, she observed a small brown bird flying away from it. It surprised her, for it seemed as though the bird flew from the approximate area of her nest. When she got to it, she knew that something was strangely different and unusual. She stood on the cup of the nest for several minutes trying to figure it out. She couldn't count and the concept of "three" was almost beyond her ability. But there were three eggs in the nest, even though she had laid only two eggs. Color gave her a clue. The fact that the third egg was not blue but was brown with darker brown speckles gave it away. The young robin's mind used these marks to detect that something was wrong in her nest and to tell her that this strange egg didn't belong here. It took her several attempts, but finally she was able to hold and push the egg with her beak, edging it over the side of the nest, where it fell through the branches of the spruce and broke even before it hit the ground.

The female Bronze-headed Cowbird witnessed the event from across the lawn. She did not return to lay another egg.

The robin deposited the third egg of the four she would lay.

As the young robin watched his mate from his resting perch midway up the big oak tree near the parking lot, he was compelled to express his happiness and ownership. For several minutes he sang, his beak pointing toward the sky, his tail moving slightly up and down in reaction to his song and the contractions of his muscles that it took to sing it. This would be the pattern of the next two weeks as life formed within the eggs. He would sing to her and watch her. Of course, he would also feed and drink. She would hardly ever leave the nest to feed and drink on her own unless he was in her sight. Then, upon leaving, she would call out and he would fly to the nest, stand on the edge, and watch over the four blue eggs resting so delicately in the bottom of the cup. On warm days she was off the nest frequently, and he would occasionally join her in feeding, bathing, and preening. On chilly days she remained on the nest for longer periods. When it was raining or misty, as it often was in early May, she would spread her wings slightly to catch the cold water and keep it from chilling the eggs.

Sometimes he even fed her, though that was not usually the case. But he would get this compulsion to hunt, even when he wasn't hungry, and he would take his prey, most often an earthworm, to the nest. His mate,

----

since she was on the nest and reluctant to leave, and since she remembered food being brought to her when she was a fledgling, responded like a juvenile, with an open, begging mouth and a fluttering of wings. This served to condition the male, preparing him for the behavior pattern he would need when the eggs hatched.

And this time the eggs would hatch. And the struggle and cycle that had given him life would be repeated, never in exactly the same way but always very similarly, to the point where the seasons of the robin have no ending, except with the termination of an individual life.

Both of the young robins will probably live three more years before succumbing. When they do die, their deaths will probably be violent, probably painful, and certainly as much a part of their lives as were their "births." Before death, their lives will have been filled with the joys of warm sunshine, plenty of berries, the pleasures of life with a flock, and the discomfort and pain of cold winters, empty stomachs, and injuries caused by fighting and weather.

Some violence is nature's way, as are some peace and happiness. One creature's sunny day is frequently another's tragic one. And that is why this story stops here. Because it never really ends. It goes on and on, changing slightly, steadily, continuously, day after day, drama after drama, robin after robin, season after season.

- - - - - - - - - - - - - - -

THE END